Aristotle's Ethics

D1057546

Aristotle's Ethics

J. O. URMSON

BLACKWELL
Oxford UK & Cambridge USA

Copyright © J. O. Urmson 1988

First published 1988
Reprinted 1989, 1991, 1993 (twice), 1994 (twice)

Blackwell Publishers, the publishing imprint of Basil Blackwell Ltd
108 Cowley Road, Oxford OX4 1JF, UK

Basil Blackwell Inc.
238 Main Street
Cambridge, Massachusetts 02142, USA

British Library Cataloguing in Publication Data

Urmson, J.O.
  Aristotle's Ethics
  1. Aristotle. Ethics 2. Ethics
  I. Title
  170 B430
ISBN 0–631–15673–9
ISBN 0–631–15946–0 pbk

Library of Congress Cataloging in Publication Data

Urmson, J.O.
  Aristotle's ethics/J.O. Urmson.
    p. cm.
  "Primarily designed to be read in conjunction with
Aristotle's Nicomachean ethics"—Pref.
  Bibliography: p.
  Includes index.
  ISBN 0–631–15673–9   ISBN 0–631–15946–0 (pbk.)
  1. Aristotle—Contributions in ethics.   2. Aristotle
Nichomachean ethics.   3. Ethics.   I. Title.
B491.E7U76 1988
171'.3—dc19   87–29367 CIP

Typeset in 10 on 12pt Garamond
by Alan Sutton Publishing, Stroud, Gloucestershire
Printed in Great Britain by
Athenæum Press, Gateshead, Tyne & Wear.

This book is printed on acid-free paper

Contents

Preface

This book is primarily designed to be read in conjunction with Aristotle's *Nicomachean Ethics* by those who are not already familiar with Aristotle's writings. It requires no knowledge of the Greek language. Some of the difficulties much discussed by professional scholars are here ignored; to others a solution is offered without reference to divergent views. Where Aristotle's text is readily comprehensible he has been left to speak for himself without comment.

The reader new to Aristotle can find his text very difficult and, indeed, intimidating, especially through the veil of a translation. This book attempts to make clear the general lines of Aristotle's thought rather than to examine the text sentence by sentence; it is offered as an aid to those who read Aristotle's own text, not as a substitute for it. There is no way to make Aristotle easy reading, but he is worth the effort.

The author has followed the ancient literary use of 'man' as a noun of common gender and the convention that the pronoun 'he' refers to persons of both sexes in the absence of contrary indications. He has not the literary skill to write otherwise without intolerable clumsiness of diction. In adopting this style he intends no offence to anyone and hopes that none will be taken.

References

All references in this book are to works of Aristotle and are incorporated in the text. General references to discussions by Aristotle are given in the form (Book I, Chapter 1). References to specific passages are of the form (1234a 12). This literally means that the passage referred to occurs on the 12th line of the left hand column of the 1234th page of Bekker's edition of the Greek text. This pagination is noted in the margins of W. D. Ross's translation of the *Nicomachean Ethics*, which is to be found in the Oxford *Works of Aristotle Translated into English*, Vol. IX, in McKeon (ed.) *Introduction to Aristotle*, and in the *World's Classics* series. Most other texts, both in Greek and English, reproduce it. Where such a reference is given not prefaced by a title, it is to the *Nicomachean Ethics*. References to other works are given in the form *(Physics* 123a 12). All translations are by the author unless otherwise attributed.

Introduction

In Homer's *Iliad* Achilles loves his friend Patroclus. The Trojan prince, Hector, kills Patroclus in battle. Achilles, enraged, kills Hector. Having killed Hector, Achilles drags his body daily around the tomb of Patroclus behind his chariot, and leaves it out at night to be mutilated by scavenger dogs. This is truly barbarous behaviour; the gods, who are not unduly squeamish, are horrified and hold a council to decide what to do about it. In the course of their debate Apollo denounces Achilles and adds: 'Let him beware lest we become angry with him, even though he is good.'

The point of this short narrative lies in the last four words: 'though he is good'; we, with our cultural background, might rather have expected: 'since he is very bad'. But Homer sees things differently. Apollo, though an enemy of the Greeks, must acknowledge that Achilles is good, for, after all, he is the son of the goddess Thetis, his father is a king, he is the greatest living warrior, he is rich, he is handsome, he is famous. No Greek of Homer's time, be he god or man, could call such a hero bad. To be bad typically involves being poor, ugly and cowardly, like Thersites in the *Iliad,* and Achilles is not like that. All men ought to be just and obey the laws of the gods, so Achilles could properly be censured, but he could not be called bad.

Homer's ideals and those of the men he wrote for were, of course, long outdated by the time of Plato and Aristotle. But still the good life was that which was to be envied, the most choiceworthy. The rule of the well born and wealthy was still called aristocracy – the rule of the best. To be good was to be enviable; to be righteous was to be praiseworthy. Unless we understand this we cannot understand Greek ethical thought.

But while goodness and righteousness were traditionally different, the great and the good were still expected to be righteous. The ideal king was just, generous and cared for his people. By Plato's time the existence of any link between goodness and righteousness had come to be questioned. In Plato's dialogues this is illustrated by such men as Polus and Callicles in the *Gorgias* and Thrasymachus in the *Republic*. In the *Republic*, when Socrates asks Thrasymachus: 'So you think that unrighteous men are sensible and good?', Thrasymachus replies: 'Yes, if they are capable of perfect unrighteousness'; the only reason for conforming to morality is fear of the consequences of not doing so. The case is perhaps best put by Glaucon and Adeimantus in Book II of the *Republic;* if you can get the praise given to the righteous by merely seeming to be righteous, what is the point of being restrained by rules of justice and fairness which are a fabrication of the many weak to protect them from the strong? Is not the best life that which affords the maximum satisfaction of one's desires, and has such a life any room for norms of behaviour that restrain that satisfaction?

Now Plato, who regarded such questioners as the main enemy, might in theory have said: 'Never mind about being happy and living the good life; never mind about your personal wellbeing; it is more important to be righteous'. But in fact he never even hints at such a line of argument. He never questions that the rational man will aim at the most worthwhile life, happiness, fulfilment. His strategy is quite different; his aim is to show that being just, being righteous, is an indispensable element in the good life, that Callicles and Thrasymachus are wrong, not for seeking the most rewarding life, but for failing to recognize what it is.

An analogy might be this: suppose that a music lover finds that those around him all agree that they want to listen to the best music; he, too, wants this, but thinks that the music that the others regard as the best is trivial, impermanent and shallow. He does not say: 'Never mind about the best music; seek the sort of music that I favour'. What he says is: 'Of course we must seek the best music, but you are mistaken about what is the best music which is in fact like this . . .'. So Plato tries to show that traditional moral excellences, such as truthfulness, piety, justice and courage, are ingredients in the best life rather than impediments to or limitations on it.

We need not suppose that Aristotle was convinced by every detail of Plato's arguments in the *Gorgias* and the *Republic*. But he accepts in his ethical writings the conclusion of those dialogues that the wise man who wishes for the best life will accept the requirements of morality. So the modern inquirer who is concerned with the arguments for and against moral scepticism, moral nihilism and moral relativism should turn to Plato rather than to Aristotle. Aristotle, as he himself says (1095b 4-8), takes it for granted that his hearers and readers will be people who have been well brought up, who do not need to be taught how to behave and who do not need to be persuaded to accept the claims of morality. He is concerned to lead us into a systematic consideration of the best way to live one's life that goes beyond what the non-philosopher, however sound in moral judgment, ever attempts. His aim is, as he often says, (for example, at 1103b 26-30), practical, but he attempts to achieve it, not by converting us from wicked ways, but by deepening our understanding. We are to be involved in an intellectual enquiry to determine what is the best sort of life, not in an attempt to convert us to an already known ideal.

If one is to lead the best sort of life, the life most worth living, one will ideally be equipped with all human excellences – excellence of character, certainly, but also excellence of intelligence, of health, of looks and of birth. Such excellences as health, good looks and good birth, though mentioned in the *Nicomachean Ethics* as desirable and elements in the best life (1099b 2-3), are not discussed there in detail; a discussion of good health, for example, would belong more properly to a biological work. But Aristotle considers it necessary to examine in careful detail excellence of character, excellence of the intelligence that is essential in practical affairs as the complement of excellence of character, and other problems of action before he is

ready for his final discussion of the good life. These are the
problems with which the major portion of the *Nicomachean Ethics*
is concerned.

Given the scope of the *Nicomachean Ethics*, as it has just been
briefly indicated, it is surely one of the best books on the
problems of conduct ever written by a philosopher. But it is also
one of the most difficult to understand correctly. Having studied
it as an undergraduate in the 1930s and having held tutorials and
seminars on it and lectured on it every year from 1946 to 1980, I
have found myself every year coming to understand, or ceasing to
misunderstand, some passage the significance of which has always
eluded me. No doubt my understanding of the text is still
imperfect, but, such as it is, I shall set it out in the following
chapters.

No doubt any philosophical text of substance is difficult and
requires hard work from the reader. But there are three main
sources of difficulty and misunderstanding in reading the *Nicomachean Ethics* not present in a typical modern philosophical text.
First, Aristotle approaches the problems of conduct from a point
of view and makes use of many concepts that are different from
those with which we are familiar today. In the English-speaking
world, whatever our personal beliefs may be, our Judeo-Christian
cultural heritage has profoundly influenced our ways of thinking;
Aristotle, writing in the fourth century BC, was untouched by
these influences. It is by no means impossible for us to come to
understand the approach of Aristotle and his Greek contem-
poraries and to come to grasp the concepts with which they
worked, but we do have to learn to do so; until we do, it is fatally
easy for us to misunderstand by quite naturally interpreting their
concepts in the light of ours. While this is a source of difficulty,
these differences are also of value, for to learn to see issues from a
new and different cultural perspective as well as our own cannot
but be an advantage. One need not suggest that Aristotle's
approach is better than ours, but it usefully stretches our minds if
we learn to comprehend it.

A second source of difficulty for us in trying to understand
Aristotle, arising in part as a consequence of the first, is the veil
of translation. When that great translator, Cicero, set himself to

give an account of Greek philosophy in Latin, he had to invent many new words and stretch the meaning of others, in order to do so. Thus, for example, he simply invented the word *qualitas*, which has become, in English, 'quality'. The pre-philosophical English language was in the same position as Latin before the time of Cicero. So the translators into English have had to imitate Cicero, and they have often done so by merely transliterating Cicero's Latin terms. Thus Cicero's translation of the Greek word *arete* was *virtus*, which in English became 'virtue', and similarly, Cicero's *vitium* was translated as 'vice'. But if we think that the words 'virtue' and 'vice' in translations of Aristotle have the meaning we should naturally expect, we shall be, and ought to be, greatly perplexed. We shall find Aristotle telling us that not enjoying eating the moderate amount of food necessary for good health is a moral vice and that it is virtuous to be good at mathematics; we shall also be surprised to learn that in Aristotle's opinion the man who overcomes temptation to misbehaviour is not virtuous. Those readers who are not so surprised have probably just failed to assimilate what they read. Now Aristotle did think that there would be something wrong with a person who could not appreciate a good healthy meal, and he did regard mathematical competence as a sign of a good intelligence, and he did think that with good training a person could come not merely to overcome temptation to misbehaviour but to cease to be tempted, and that this was an improvement, but the translations are certainly liable to puzzle and mislead.

No doubt the difficulties caused by translation can be partly removed by better translation; for example, it would be well to remove the words 'virtue' and 'vice' from the translation and replace them by, say, 'excellence' and 'flaw'. But translation, however excellent, can never avoid some degree of difficulty of the kind illustrated above. No doubt all translation is subject to this difficulty, not only translation from Aristotle. But translation of abstract discussions, such as philosophy, must always present special difficulties. If Aristotle could be brought back to life and taught German he would probably find it an impossible task to make head or tail of Kant's ethical works, while to translate Kant into ancient Greek would be quite impossible.

Anthropologists can be very severely tested in their attempts to understand totally alien cultures and thought processes. Ancient Greek thought is not thus totally alien, for Hellenic influences on our culture are as basic as those of Judaism and Christianity; but, nonetheless, Greek texts can present problems of the same type as those faced by anthropologists, and we must always be wary lest we reinterpret them in the light of more recent thought.

A third main difficulty in understanding the *Nicomachean Ethics* arises from the nature of the text itself. Very few competent critics have ever doubted that, with the exception of a few editorial phrases of no importance, the work is a genuine representation of Aristotle's thought. But, even more evidently in the Greek than in most translations, it is not a finished and continuous literary text. How it came to be as it is nobody knows. A plausible guess is that it is a set of notes written by Aristotle as a basis for his lectures, and perhaps intended to be deposited in the school library for consultation by members. Indications of this are such expressions in the text as 'as we also said the other day' (1104b 18) and 'as can be gathered from the diagram' (1107a 33), which diagram was presumably written on the Greek equivalent of a blackboard, since there is no diagram in the text. There are also cryptic allusions such as that to the man who let fly with a catapult when he intended only to display it (1111a 10), which would presumably have been expanded in a lecture. Others have, less plausibly in my view, conjectured that what we have is lecture notes by a member of the audience; we have no source for any opinion on this topic save conjecture.

It is very hard to doubt that the text is by Aristotle, but it very clearly was not written as a continuous unity, which is another source of difficulty. Thus Books V, VI and VII of the *Nicomachean Ethics* are also Books IV, V and VI of the *Eudemian Ethics* and stylistic evidence suggests that they were originally part of the *Eudemian Ethics*. A possible explanation is that Aristotle revised some topics and not others, so that editors made the unrevised portion part of two otherwise different editions. That editors did join together into a whole manuscripts of Aristotle not so unified by him himself is quite evident. Thus the last few chapters of Book VII are on pleasure and end with the words: 'It remains for us to discuss friendship'. Friendship is duly discussed in books VIII and IX, while Book IX ends with the words: 'The next thing to discuss is pleasure', and pleasure receives a treatment at the beginning of Book X which is quite independent of that in Book VII. It is plausible to conjecture that pious editors thus roughly put together manuscripts of the great man which they were unwilling to abandon.

Classical scholars have a fine time arguing the details of these matters. We need merely note that the text is not a unity and accept the common verdict that the text of the *Nicomachean Ethics* is all genuine Aristotle, though not a single treatise. All professional philosophers have written separate papers and revised lecture notes on different aspects of their subject, and have often treated the same theme two or three times. If the books on friendship were originally an independent essay, while the *Nicomachean* and *Eudemian Ethics* were alternative treatments of the same subject matter which editors posthumously conflated in part, nobody should be surprised.

Thus, apart from the inherent difficulties of the subject matter, the text may be difficult to understand from any one, or any combination of, the three causes that have been outlined above. It may be that the text presupposes unfamiliar concepts and cultural outlooks; it may be that the translation misleads us; it may be that Aristotle himself fails to give us the explanations and clarifications that we could reasonably expect from a unitary text prepared by the author for publication. The remedies for these difficulties, though not always easy to apply, are plain. The concepts and cultural presuppositions, even if at times somewhat unfamiliar, are neither mysterious nor ineffable. They can be described and explained. Where translations tend to be opaque or misleading, paraphrase and alternative translations can be helpful. Where the text is cryptic and overconcise, we can draw on our familiarity with Aristotle's thought, on parallel texts and on the wisdom of generations of commentators. There will remain passages the meaning of which, to me at least, will still be doubtful. But on the whole an original, penetrating and substantial body of thought can be elicited from the text of the *Nicomachean Ethics* which is well worth the labour involved in coming to understand it.

Finally, a note for the curious on the name 'Nicomachean Ethics'. Aristotle had a son named Nicomachus, who was still a child when his father died and is said to have been killed young in battle; he is not known to have been a philosopher. What connexion this fact has with the title is not known. The French call the work *L'Ethique à Nicomaque,* thus suggesting that the work was addressed or dedicated to his infant son by its author; the cover of the *World's Classics* edition says that the work was 'so called after their first editor, Aristotle's son Nicomachus', which is an implausible conjecture without any evidence to support it. In fact, nobody knows why the work is called the *Nicomachean Ethics,* just as nobody knows why the *Eudemian Ethics* is so called, though it is known that Aristotle had a pupil named Eudemus who came from Rhodes.

1

The Ideal Life: a Preliminary Discussion

Many Aristotelian texts begin with a vast generalization, and the *Nicomachean Ethics* is one of them. 'Every art, procedure, action and undertaking aims at some good', says Aristotle (1094a 1). We might wish to object to this. More seriously, we might point out that some ends that seem desirable to some people sometimes are in fact bad; Aristotle will deal with that point later on. Less seriously, we might query whether twiddling one's thumbs, and doodling, for example, aim at anything, good or bad. It would therefore be as well to notice at once a warning given by Aristotle early in the *Nicomachean Ethics* on the nature and method of his inquiry (1094b 11). Accuracy, he tells us, is a function of the subject matter of an inquiry; in mathematics total accuracy and precision is the norm; in many other areas generalizations have to be more or less rough and sketchy, and there will always be exceptions. Thus as generalizations 'It is a good thing to be rich' and 'It is a good thing to be brave' are considered by Aristotle to be obvious truths at the level of accuracy of which ethical discussion is capable; but, as he points out, 'both wealth and bravery can destroy a man' (1094b 16-18). It is, he tells us in one of those pithy observations at which he excels, 'a mark of the educated man to demand accuracy only to the degree that the subject-matter permits' (1094b 24-25). The *Nicomachean Ethics* is an inquiry in a field where all our generalizations must be approximate.

So we can agree with Aristotle that on the whole whatever

people do it will be for the sake of something good, or at least what they think is worth aiming at. The essential point is that generally when a person does something there will be an answer to the question why he is doing it. Action in general is not pointless. But there is an important distinction to be made; some things that we do we do for their own sake, other things we do in order to bring about something beyond the action itself (1094a 4–5). Perhaps we listen to music, or wander round art galleries because that is the sort of thing we want to do; it is an end in itself. But most people catch trains only in order to reach some destination and make cakes only because they want to eat them. The chain can be much longer; we plough fields in order to grow wheat, which we do to get the grain, which we grind to get flour, which we bake to make bread, which we make in order to eat it. Perhaps we could continue that chain still further; we eat to assuage our hunger, for example. But Aristotle is surely right in claiming that the chain must have a final link that there must be something which is an end desired for its own sake (1094a 21–22).

At this point Aristotle makes a suggestion that causes difficulty: might there not be some end for the sake of which everything is done, at which all action aims? The first difficulty is that it looks suspiciously as if Aristotle moves from the obvious truth, that every action has some end, to the claim that there is some end at which all action aims; this is no more justifiable than the move from 'Every nice girl loves a sailor' to 'There is a sailor whom every nice girl loves'. If we can find no better ground for accepting Aristotle's suggestion, we had better not accept it at all. But a bad argument for a conclusion does not falsify the conclusion.

However, a more potent difficulty is that Aristotle himself has already agreed that there are many things which we do for their own sake and many ulterior ends at which we aim; he has mentioned health, victory and wealth as such ulterior ends in his first few lines, and we surely do not usually listen to music as a means to some further end, though we might listen to a piece of music as a means to passing a music examination. It is important to see how Aristotle can answer this objection, for in seeing this we shall also see Aristotle's basic reason for thinking that the wise man will have one final end in life. We already have before us the distinction between an activity undertaken for its own sake and one undertaken as a means to some end; we must now make a further distinction and recognize a class of actions that are both ends in themselves and also constituents in (not means to) some wider end.

We might imagine a person who is dancing and who is doing so for its own sake and not, say, purely for health reasons. Let us now consider each individual step in the dance and ask whether it is being performed for its own sake. If we were to say that each step was being taken simply as a means to dancing, it would seem to follow that none of the dance was being done for its own sake. It seems more plausible to say that, just because the dancer is dancing for the sake of dancing, each element in the dance is performed for its own sake. As he performs each motion it will be equally true to say that he is doing it for its own sake or for the sake of dancing. Each movement is an end in itself and a constituent in the dance, which is also the end.

If we recognize this class of activities that are ends in themselves but also constituents in a wider end, the difficulty we raised will disappear and we shall be better placed to understand Aristotle's suggestion. He is suggesting that we may have some widest, all-embracing, end so that the things we do for their own sake are all partially constitutive of that widest end. If that is so, it is worthwhile for us to decide what that all-embracing end should be, for it must be the greatest good of all (1094a 23).

At this stage (1095a 18), Aristotle says that there is such a supreme end and that everyone agrees what it is, so far as words go. They all agree that the right name for it is 'eudaemonia'. This Greek word, now part of the English language, is often translated as 'happiness'; everyone agrees that this translation is misleading, but many accept it because they cannot think of a better. It is safer merely to transliterate and to explain the meaning. This is very easy to do since Aristotle tells us that everyone agrees that 'eudaemonia' means the same as 'living and faring well' (1905a 19–20). So to say that somebody is *eudaemon* is the very same thing as to say that he is living a life worth living. It is emphatically not to say, as might be the case when one describes somebody as happy, that he is, at the time of speaking, feeling on top of the world, or any other way. To call somebody *eudaemon* is to judge his life as a whole, so that a cautious man, as Solon advised, will not call anybody *eudaemon* until he is dead. This, says Aristotle (1100a 10–15), is not the absurd view that one is never well off while alive, but only when one is in the grave, but the cautious view that it is not safe to judge a life as the sort of life that is worth living until one has seen the whole of it. To call a person *eudaemon* while he is still alive is like calling a book a good book when one has still only read part of it – it is not safe, though, of course, people do it. But, says Aristotle, when one calls a young person *eudaemon* it is a forecast on the basis of a favourable start, not a final judgment (1100a 1–4). It is clear that this notion of eudaemonia is different from ours of happiness.

But if to be *eudaemon* is to live a good life, we must not interpret this saying as a moral judgment. Aristotle himself does hold that the best life will be one which, among other things, exhibits excellence of character. But to be *eudaemon* is to be well off, to have what is most desirable, not to be praiseworthy. Just as a games player will probably find his games more satisfying if he plays without cheating, so with life as a whole. The notion of being of good character even though one's life is thereby circumscribed and diminished is not one which any Greek held.

If one lives a moral life one is, no doubt, to be praised. If one lives the *eudaemon* life one is to be congratulated. Aristotle frequently makes the distinction between what is to be prized and what is to be praised (e.g. 1101b 10), and eudaemonia is to be prized. It is a success, an achievement. If one asks the question of the modern moralist: 'How ought I to live?' one is not asking Aristotle's question: 'What is the *eudaemon* life?'. Aristotle's question requires an answer more like that required to the question asked of a parent: 'What sort of life do you hope for your children?' Parents, in general, want their children to succeed in life, though they have different views of what constitutes success. So had the Greeks.

Once the nature of the inquiry becomes clear we can understand why Aristotle is so certain that there must be one single final end of life and does not bother to argue the case with any care. The decisive point is this: let us imagine an objector who claims that eudaemonia would be improved if we added to it the element X, so that the double end of eudaemonia plus X would be superior to the single end of eudaemonia. Aristotle's answer to this would be that this is merely a misleading way of saying that X is an element in eudaemonia. So, if we envisage the ideal life, omitting nothing that could improve it, we have envisaged eudaemonia; so how could there be a further end? Certainly we want honour, pleasure and every possible excellence, says Aristotle, and we want them for their own sake (1097b 2). But, since they are, in Aristotle's own words, 'parts of eudaemonia' (1129b 18), we can also say that we want them in order to live the ideal life, whereas it would be absurd to say that we want to live the ideal life in order to achieve anything else. Eudaemonia is the one thing we not only choose for its own sake but cannot choose for the sake of anything else (1097b 1).

Thus it is clear that eudaemonia is not just one element in the ideal life. It is clear also that eudaemonia is composite; the ideal life is not made ideal by just one element that it contains, but has multiple criteria or desiderata. Aristotle, whose feet were on earth and whose head, despite his intellectual eminence, was not in the clouds, even holds that one cannot be altogether *eudaemon* if one is very ugly, lowborn, solitary or childless (1095b 2–5). One also needs money (1099a 31–34). Certainly pleasure, friendship and all human excellences are requisite. Aristotle even entertains the possibility that what happens after one's death can affect one's eudaemonia, not because one may suffer in hell or rejoice in heaven, or even because one might beyond the grave be aware of what goes on in the world, but because nobody would want to be the sort of person whose children turn out to be rascals, even after one's death (1100a 10–30).

The point that the ideal is complex is well made in the *Magna Moralia*, a work traditionally ascribed to Aristotle, though many doubt its authenticity. The perspicacious author of the *Magna Moralia*, whoever he may be, wrote: 'But the ideal that we are now seeking is not simple. For example, someone might say that wisdom is the greatest of all goods, taken separately. But perhaps we should not seek the highest good in that way. For we are seeking the complete good, and wisdom on its own is incomplete'. We find also in the *Magna Moralia* the sentence: 'For eudaemonia is a composite of certain good things. For eudaemonia is nothing apart from these, but these'. Whoever the author, this is sound Aristotelian doctrine.

I have laboured this point because Aristotle sometimes talks as though he did wish to identify eudaemonia with that one element, wisdom, that the *Magna Moralia* says is not the ideal but is, on its own, incomplete, Thus he begins Chapter 6 of Book X by saying that, after discussing excellence, friendship and pleasure, the time has come to discuss eudaemonia in outline (1176a 30–32), and he ends Chapter VIII with the judgment that the life of contemplative thought is the most *eudaemon* (1178a 6–7). He also speaks of the life in which one gives scope to the exercise of excellences of character and practical wisdom as a second best (1178a 9–10). This has, not surprisingly, caused puzzlement and led to charges of inconsistency against Aristotle. Does he, it is asked, wish to make eudaemonia the inclusive or the dominant end of life? But I think that the explanation is quite simple and that there is no real inconsistency. The elements in eudaemonia, as conceived by Aristotle, are compatible with and desirable in any sort of life. High birth, good looks and the like may be more important to the politician than to the scholar, but are not to be despised by anybody. But certain life styles are incompatible; one might hanker after being a great musician, a great Aristotelian scholar or a prime minister. None of these are unworthy ambitions, but they are not compatible and one must choose; Paderewski's piano playing deteriorated when he became prime minister of Poland and Gladstone's philosophical work is sparse and mediocre. Some choices determine one's whole way of life and exclude many others. Aristotle's view is that a life of public activity and a life of intellectual contemplation are the two main contenders for the place of the best life style and that one has to choose. The one gives scope to practical excellence, the other to theoretical excellence. He makes his choice; one may not agree with it, but I do not think that he is guilty of incon-sistency. One can, perhaps, complain that he did not make things clearer, but any criticism should be suspended until one has seen his grounds for coming to the final conclusion in Book X.

So much for our explanation of the notion of eudaemonia, which Aristotle tells us is agreed by everyone to be the name of the best kind of life and means the same as to live and fare well. But he goes on immediately (1095a 20–22) to say that they disagree about what it is, and to mention some current views, such as that it is pleasure or honour. Commentators have puzzled much over the interpretation of this question. 'What is eudaemonia?' is a question in the standard form: 'What is X?' in which Aristotle asks for a definition – in the sense in which he uses the word so translated. If we confuse an Aristotelian definition with what we now call a definition – a formula giving the meaning of a word to be defined – we shall properly be puzzled, since Aristotle has already told us that everyone agrees that 'eudaemonia' means the same as 'living and faring well'. Moreover Aristotle tells us that some people believe that the answer to the question: 'What is eudaemonia?' is 'Honour'; but nobody could suppose that 'honour' means the same as 'eudaemonia'. Our puzzlement will vanish if we recognize that an Aristotelian definition is not intended to give the meaning of a word.

An Aristotelian definition is not anything very mysterious, though the traditional formula that it gives the essence of the thing defined sounds very portentous. Perhaps it would be better to say that a definition tells us what the thing defined really is. Let us consider one of the examples that Aristotle uses when explaining definition in his *Analytics*. What is an eclipse? Everyone knows the meaning of the word – an eclipse is the temporary ending of the light of the sun or of the moon. But it remains sensible to ask: 'What *is* an eclipse?' To this question some have thought that the correct answer was that the moon had been swallowed by a dragon. But Greek astronomers had discovered that an eclipse (of the moon) was the interposition of the earth between the sun and the moon. This, Aristotle tells us, is the definition of an eclipse. So in this case the definition is given not, of course, by the lexicographer, nor by a metaphysician with some mysterious insight, but by a scientist. So it seems that the answer required to the question: 'What is an eclipse?' will have the nature of an explanation, one that gives us an understanding of the phenomenon – not of the word, which we have already.

Not all 'What is X?' questions will require a scientific answer. 'What is a good motor car?' can be answered well only by somebody with technological competence, but is not a scientific, or even a technological, question. The answer to it will enable us to judge and choose between motor cars. 'What is eudaemonia?' is in some respects a similar question. It is a demand for the criteria by which to judge and choose between different kinds of life. To answer the question well we need to be able to think philosophically, but it is not a theoretical but a practical problem. How to set about answering the question we shall find out, according to Aristotle, by reading the *Ethics*.

The first clue on how to set about answering the question is given at 1095b 2–9. There is a procedure from first principles, where we start from perhaps very abstract axioms or fundamental truths, which may be difficult to understand and remote from everyday thought, but which are self-evident in the sense that they require and admit no prior justification; we then draw conclusions from these and end up with something quite specific with which we are already familiar. Thus, perhaps, starting from the abstract first principles of Newtonian mechanics we deduce that an apple will fall to the ground when no longer attached to its tree. But there is another sort of procedure in which we move towards first principles and start from what is familiar to us. It would seem that this is how 'Newton got to his first principles, and it is hard to imagine how else he would have arrived at them. In ethical inquiries, Aristotle tells us, we have to start in this second way from what is familiar to us.

But in ethics we cannot start from visible occurrences, such as apples falling from trees, for we are concerned with values and not with simple empirical facts. What we have to start from, he tells us, is what is said about conduct by everyone, or by the majority, or by the wise (Book I, Chapter 8 *passim*). These current views may, on reflection, need to be clarified, guarded, modified and, when they disagree with one another, reconciled. But rather as J.S. Mill thought it absurd to deny that what everybody desired was desirable, so Aristotle accepted common assent as cogent in ethical enquiries. 'What seems true to everyone, that we say is the case' (1173a 1).

We can find a parallel, in spite of the difference between modern and ancient philosophy, in modern moral philosophy. There are those who, following Aristotle's first procedure from first principles, construct a moral system on the basis of some basic principle which they claim to be luminously self-evident. If commonly accepted moral beliefs do not accord with the system, then they need to be reformed. Such has been the practice of many utilitarians, who start from a principle of maximization of general welfare and regard all other moral principles and decisions as subordinate to and derivable from it. On the other hand, there are those who regard the job of the moral philosopher as being to take the common moral consensus as the datum and to endeavour to set out what order and system they can find in the various judgements of the unphilosophical moral agents around them. Aristotle is not constructing a moral philosophy in the modern sense; but there is a parallel between the procedure that he advocates and that of the latter type of moral philosopher.

Such at least is Aristotle's professed method, and it is one that he follows most of the time. He even goes so far as to say: 'For if difficulties are resolved and accepted opinions remain, that is sufficient demonstration' (1145b 6–7). We shall often find him, however, going beyond this cautious goal. We shall also find him using an occasional a priori argument, though when he does so he is always careful to show that the conclusion so arrived at is supported by accepted beliefs.

Most of the rest of Book 1 of the *Nicomachean Ethics* is devoted to giving not a complete but a preliminary answer to this question: 'What is eudaemonia?' which is the central question that Aristotle sets out to answer in this work. It might even be held that it is not even an outline answer, but rather an indication of how and where the answer is to be sought. In one of the formulations of this answer we are told that the good for man is 'activity of the soul exhibiting the highest and most complete excellence in a complete life' (1098a 15–18). This answer, which certainly requires elucidation in the translation I have given it, is made more difficult and even misleading in the standard translations, which make Aristotle say that the good for man is 'activity in accordance with virtue' instead of 'activity exhibiting excellence'. What Aristotle is saying is not that the central element in eudaemonia is activity that remains within the bounds of morality, but that a life devoted to even the most worthwhile activities carried out rather badly will be less choiceworthy than one in which the same activities are conducted at the peak of efficiency. If playing snooker were to turn out to be the most worthwhile of all human activities, it would be best to be a first-class snooker player. Aristotle's own illustration is that if one is going to play the aulos (a reedpipe), one had better play it well (1098a 9–10). Aristotle is, in Book X, going to single out contemplation of immutable truth as the most worthwhile of all activities. One cannot carry out this activity either virtuously or viciously; but one can do it better or worse, and it is more worthwhile to do it better.

But in Book I Aristotle does not claim only that the central criterion of eudaemonia, the good life, is the activities that it includes; he also tells us that these activities will involve the use of reason (1098a 13–15). So the most complete preliminary account of eudaemonia will be that it is activity involving the use of reason, at a high level of excellence and throughout a complete life. We must remember, of course, that there are always subsidiary considerations, such as good looks and others mentioned at 1099b 3–5.

If we examine the reasons that Aristotle gives for this account of eudaemonia, we shall find that for the most part they are common-sense and widely held considerations. We shall note three of them:

1   The worthwhileness of a type of life must depend on the actions it contains rather than merely on the abilities and character that it manifests. A life of a person who had the most excellent disposition but who was always asleep like Rip van Winkle would not be worth much.

2   We think that the value of a man's life is largely in his own
    power to determine. Many of the things that happen to a
    man for better or worse are out of his control; but he can to
    a great extent choose his own actions. So if eudaemonia is
    to be, short of calamities, within our power to achieve, it
    should depend largely on our actions.

3   The three types of life commonly put forward as candidates
    for supremacy are the life of sensual pleasure, the life of
    involvement in the affairs of one's country and the life of
    theoretical contemplation. The first of these is the aim of a
    mere animal; the other two must include activity invol-
    ving the use of reason, either practical or theoretical.

These three considerations, and some others mentioned by
Aristotle, are all designed to show that his preliminary account of
eudaemonia fits in with our common beliefs; they are of the
second type mentioned by Aristotle, moving towards, rather
than from first principles. But there is a further argument of a
more metaphysical type which is liable, perhaps with good
reason, to worry the modern reader. This is an argument based on
the claim that man has a function. This function is then said to
be the use of reason, so that the life that does not include the
fulfilment of this function will be incomplete and imperfect.
From this it is concluded that the best life must be one of rational
activity. This argument is to be found at 1097b 23–1098a 10.

This argument meets with two kinds of objection. The first of
these objections denies that man has a function. Aristotle says
(1097b 25–28) that if the aulos player and the sculptor have
functions, as they clearly do, then surely man must have one too.
But the obvious reply is that 'sculptor' is indeed a functional
term, like 'screwdriver' or 'steering wheel', but 'man', 'horse' and
the like are not functional terms. Man may use the horse for
certain purposes, but this shows only that man is the imperialist
of the animal kingdom, not that the horse, of its own nature, has
a function to fulfill.

This objection, even when put thus briefly, is perhaps
irresistible, but we can perhaps try to appreciate Aristotle's
viewpoint. As a biologist, Aristotle had come to the conclusion

that nature is purposive. We can, he thinks, inquire into the function of the heart, the liver, the kidneys or the eye and expect to find an answer; none of these organs are mere useless superfluities. But while man, in common with all other animals has a heart, kidneys, liver, eyes and the like, he alone has the capacity to reason. This distinguishing feature cannot be a mere useless superfluity either; it is what makes a person distinctively human and so the fully human life must include it. This purposive view of nature is, of course, frowned on nowadays by theorists of scientific method, though if we are honest we may find it hard to claim that it is entirely absent from our own thought.

The second of the common objections mentioned above is that even if we accept that a perfect specimen of a human life must include the use of reason, this will show only that this is the good of man not the good for man. Man, it is suggested, might be better off if he were to neglect his distinctively human capacities. If Aristotle is claiming to provide a deductive proof that reason is part of the best life he has, perhaps, no answer to this objection. But I think that Aristotle would answer that a life that left out this distinctively human activity of reasoning would be the choice of men 'slavish in their tastes, preferring a life suitable to beasts' (1095b 19–20). Like Satan in Milton's *Paradise Lost* he would say:

> For who would lose,
> Though full of pain, this intellectual being,
> These thoughts that wander through eternity.

It is, however, clear that this reply cannot on its own justify the very central role that Aristotle will assign to reason and contemplation in the final chapters of the *Nicomachean Ethics*; Aristotle will bring forward new arguments to that conclusion which we must evaluate when we come to them.

From this preliminary sketch of eudaemonia, according to which its central criterion is activity exhibiting excellence and involving the use of reason, the bulk of the rest of the *Nicomachean Ethics* derives. The key terms are 'action', 'excellence' and 'reason': in Book II Aristotle will discuss excellence of character; in the first part of Book III and again in the earlier part of Book VII he will discuss action and responsibility; in the latter part of Book III and in Books IV and V he will discuss particular excellences of character such as bravery and justice; in Book VI he discusses excellence in reasoning, both theoretical and practical.

Aristotle recognizes three types of human excellence: bodily excellence, excellence of character and excellence of intelligence. Bodily excellence.is, as we have seen, to at least some degree essential to eudaemonia, for if one is ugly or diseased one is impaired to some degree. But bodily excellence is a topic for biological and medical study rather than having a place in an ethical work, so Aristotle does not discuss it in detail in the *Nicomachean Ethics*. The other two types of excellence he does discuss in detail. If eudaemonia is predominantly determined by activity displaying excellence, Aristotle will first examine the nature and varieties of human excellence and then, finally in Book X, consider what activity or activities should be central in the best human life.

Both types of excellence, that of character and that of intelligence, fall within the rational life of man and are within the sphere where choice is possible. Excellences of intelligence, such as planning ability and theoretical insight, are rational eminently and in themselves; excellences of character, though in themselves not forms of intelligence, not, as Aristotle himself puts it, excellences of the rational but of a non-rational part of the soul, still 'listen to reason' (1102b 30). By listening to reason excellence of character differs from bodily excellence. To use a biblical example, 'no man by taking thought can add one cubit to his stature', nor can he decide to become better looking or more healthy, though he might decide to visit a cosmetic surgeon or change his diet in the hope that improved looks or health will result. But we can decide to become more abstemious in bodily indulgence, we can decide to behave well or badly and in general to behave in accordance with the dictates of reason. So in studying excellence of action we shall have to study its two distinguishable but inseparable aspects, excellence of disposition or character and that kind of thinking which is concerned with and controls (or should control) our choices. Aristotle will study excellence of character first, and while reading that study we must never forget that it is only one element in good action. A study of excellence of character does not try to answer the question what is the best way to act or the question how we should make our choice of action; it is concerned only with the question what sort of character is needed if sound choices are to be made. Only thought can determine what course of action is best on any occasion; excellence of character has the sole, but important, role of making the agent willing to do what reason determines is the best course of action. If we remember this, Aristotle's account of excellence of character and his celebrated doctrine of the mean will present no difficulty, except on a few points of detail. If we forget it, and most traditional accounts of the matter do forget it, we shall totally misunderstand both the account and the doctrine.

APPENDIX

Our discussion of the central topics of Book I of the *Nicomachean Ethics* has completely ignored Chapter 6. The reason for this is that this difficult and often obscure discussion of Platonic doctrine is purely negative and contributes nothing to Aristotle's positive thesis. Since it is famous and not without interest a little will be said about it now; but this section of the chapter can be passed over by those who so wish without detriment to their understanding of Aristotle's own doctrines.

In Books V and VI of Plato's *Republic* the class of Guardians is said to live the most *eudaemon* life possible, and the supreme element in their eudaemonia is said to be their attainment, after long and arduous preparation, of the vision of the form of the good. Chapter 6 of Book I is an attack on this view. As Aristotle understands him, at least, Plato regards the forms as self-subsistent paradigms, prior to, separate from and more real than the empirical world which is only a copy or reflection of them. Aristotle does not deny merely the existence of such a form of the good; he denies that there are any forms answering to this description. According to Aristotle, the form or universal, like matter, is an abstraction from the only true reality, which is a composite of matter and form. Thus the shape or form of a piece of wax cannot exist independently of the wax or some other matter, nor can the piece of wax exist without displaying some form or other.

Aristotle's serious attacks on the separate, paradigmatic form are to be found in his *Metaphysics*, and there is little, if anything, in Chapter 6 that adds to them. The interest of this chapter lies elsewhere. In general, Aristotle would agree with Plato that, when we call a set of things by the same name, it is because they share a single universal form. Thus all red things exhibit the same universal redness and all men exhibit the form of humanity. Aristotle merely denies that there is a form of red or a form of man that is a paradigm existing independently of the individuals that exhibit them. But in this chapter he denies, not merely that there is a separate Platonic form of the good, but even that there is a single universal goodness that is exhibited by all good things, a much more radical claim.

Aristotle's arguments to this effect are obscure in detail and depend on his doctrine of categories in their formulation. Basically, what he claims is that a good substance, such as God, a good quality, such as wisdom, a good quantity, and so on through the categories, are utterly disparate in their nature. Substance, quality and quantity are ultimate types of being and do not share a common character. There is no single universal being and no single universal goodness. Perhaps an analogy from time and place, two other Aristotelian categories, may help understanding. We may speak of a long time and of a long distance; but it is not clear that there is one single sort of length that can be ascribed to both a time and a distance. If we can understand a denial of this, perhaps we shall also understand why Aristotle thinks that when we call God good and the weather good we are not attributing a common characteristic to them.

Thus the term 'good', like the term 'being' is not univocal. But Aristotle recognizes that to call both a quality and a quantity good is not a mere pun, as when we call both a blow and a certain party drink a punch. He suggests intermediate possibilities: 'Are goods one, then, by being derived from one good or by all contributing to one good, or are they rather one by analogy?' (1096b 26–28). These obscure sounding phrases are easily explained in the light of Aristotle's other writings. Being derived from one case can be exemplified by the term 'healthy'. A healthy person, a healthy diet and a healthy complexion do not exhibit a common characteristic, 'health'. But there is no pun involved; the central case, the person and the others are all called healthy because the diet contributes to and the complexion manifests the health of the person. 'All contributing to one good' is the same thing looked at from the other end; the diet and the complexion contribute, each in its own way, to the health of the person.

The notion of analogy is one that became very important in mediaeval theology. 'Analogy' is a Greek mathematical term for what we call proportion, such as a:b :: c:d. The classic illustration is that we can speak both of the foot of a man and the foot of a mountain because, in spite of their manifest dissimilarities, the foot of the mountain stands in the same relation to the mountain as the foot of the man stands to the man. Aristotle does not tell us in detail how these suggestions are to be applied to the case of goodness; he merely points out that pure synonymity and pure homonymity are not the only two possibilities to consider.

Aristotle's preliminary remark in this chapter that it is distasteful to attack the theory of forms because it was introduced by friends seems somewhat belied by the style of his discussion. At one place in the *Metaphysics* he says that to call forms paradigms and to say that things participate in them is 'empty verbiage and poetic metaphor'. Aristotle does not seem to try very hard to pull his punches.

2

Excellence of Character

One of the main topics discussed in Plato's ethical dialogues, notably the *Meno*, is how excellence (or virtue, as the translations usually say) is acquired. Especially the question asked is whether it can be taught. Aristotle begins Book II of the *Nicomachean Ethics* with a dogmatic, but clearly correct, answer to the question which well illustrates his very frequent way of solving problems by making distinctions. Excellences of intelligence, he says, are largely acquired by teaching; excellences of character, being nonrational, cannot be taught but are acquired by training (the translations often say 'by habituation', but excellence of character is not a mere matter of habit, such as putting on one sock before another when dressing). We have, of course, to be born with the relevant capacities if we are to acquire excellences, whether of character or of intelligence, as most men to some degree are, but the excellence has to be developed.

We must not misunderstand this. Aristotle does not mean that we are born bad, antisocial, creatures of original sin, and that training will convert us from being bad into being good. Aristotle believes that we are born without any character at all. If we are normal human beings and not naturally incapacitated by some abnormal defect, then whether we acquire a good or a bad character depends on the kind of upbringing we get. He is evidently more impressed by the effects of environment than those of heredity, though in Book X he acknowledges that we can be better or worse disposed to respond to good training, as different soils better or worse nourish the seed (1179b 20–26).

Aristotle compares acquiring a good character with acquiring a skill. Paradoxical though it may sound, one learns to play the piano by playing the piano, and to ride a bicycle by riding one. Before one has acquired the art or skill one acts in accordance with the instructions of a teacher, who tells us what to do, and one does it with effort. Gradually, by practice and repetition, it becomes effortless and second nature. In the same way, one is trained as a child (if lucky in one's parents and teachers) to become truthful, generous, fair and the like by being told how to behave well and encouraged to do so. Parents supply the intelligence and experience that one has not yet developed, and with practice and repetition it becomes easier and easier to follow their counsel. A child who has been trained to share his toys with his friends finds it easier and easier to do so; the child who has not been so trained will find it hard and will resent having to do so. Such is Aristotle's view, and surely he is right. At the same time, he believes, one's practical intelligence will develop so that one will less and less need parents and guardians to tell one how to behave in various circumstances; one will come to see for oneself. Aristotle also echoes Plato, mentioning him by name (1104b 12), in insisting that correct training is not coercion. If properly trained one comes to enjoy doing things the right way, to want to do things the right way, and to be distressed by doing things wrongly.

We must now notice a very important sentence from Chapter 3 of Book II, first in a typical translation, then in my own. It is the passage from 1104b 13–16:

> If the virtues are concerned with actions and passions, and every passion and every action is accompanied by pleasure and pain, for this reason also virtue will be concerned with pleasures and pains.
>
> (Ross)

> If excellences are concerned with actions and emotions, and every emotion and every action involves liking or dislike, for this reason excellence will be concerned with one's likes and dislikes.
>
> (J.O.U.)

Ross's translation is not, of course, wrong, but it can mislead the unwary. What Aristotle is saying is that whether one has an excellent character or not depends not merely on what one does but also on what one likes doing. If a person acts generously there may be many explanations, some discreditable; if one regularly acts generously because one likes acting generously, if one is emotionally inclined towards generosity, then one has an excellent character in this area of action. So character depends rather on what one likes doing, what one enjoys doing, what one wants to do, than merely on what one does. The man of excellent character will act effortlessly in the correct way; he will not have to make himself so act.

Here we have one more reason for preferring to talk of excellence of character rather than of moral virtue. An illustration will help to make the point clear. Let us suppose that Brown is a strong, healthy, extrovert, full of self-confidence. He is at a meeting where a course of action which he believes to be wrong is very popular with the majority; he speaks out against the policy and has no difficulty in doing so. Let us suppose that Smith, a shy, retiring, hesitant person, is also at the meeting and also disapproves of the popular view. He can bring himself to speak out against it only by a great and very disagreeable effort of will. Perhaps we may agree that Smith is the man who has displayed the moral virtue of courage; if you were to compliment Brown on his courage he would not have the faintest idea what you were talking about. But for Aristotle, Brown is the man who has excellence of character; he is the man who acts effortlessly and as he wants to act, without any internal friction. Aristotle is not making a hopelessly wrong judgment about moral virtue; he is raising a different sort of question. The excellent character is that which a man will have who lives the most *eudaemon* life, the most choiceworthy life. If we were to ask, not for what sort of person do we feel most moral respect, but what sort of person we should wish a child of ours to be, we shall be nearer to Aristotle's viewpoint. He thinks a parent should aim to train his or her children to behave properly without effort.

Another way in which the rendering of Aristotle's text as saying that moral virtue is concerned with pleasures and pains is liable to mislead is this. There is, indeed, one area of excellence of character which is properly concerned with pleasure, temperance, and one concerned with pain, endurance. The temperate man enjoys, likes, wants sensual pleasure (food, drink, sex) only to the degree appropriate and the man of endurance does not flinch from pain when the situation demands that he endure it. No doubt it is going too far to say that he enjoys it (remember that Aristotle is speaking generally and in outline), but he does not want to act otherwise in spite of the pain; there is no internal conflict. So on the whole we are less liable to misinterpret Aristotle if we use the language of likes, enjoyment, wants, and their contraries rather than that of pleasure and pain when talking of excellence of character in general and not specifically of temperance.

But, the reader may well ask, surely it is possible for us, like the imaginary Smith voicing unpopular views with difficulty, to act properly when we do not want to, and has Aristotle forgotten this? Aristotle has not forgotten this, and there is a careful discussion of this possibility in Book VII. Perhaps Aristotle would have been more helpful to us had he not postponed his discussion of this possibility to so late in the work – if indeed the arrangement of the work is his.

So excellence of character is a settled disposition to want to act and to act in a way appropriate to the situation. What way is appropriate must, of course, be determined by reason; excellence of character can merely ensure willing compliance with the requirements of practical thinking. But Aristotle has more to tell us about excellence of character; most importantly, there is his celebrated doctrine of the mean, which is part of his definition of excellence of character, and it is to the doctrine of the mean that we shall now turn our attention.

Few philosophical theories have been more frequently and more grossly misunderstood, in my opinion, than the doctrine of the mean. Readers are therefore warned that the exposition that they find here will most probably differ greatly from those they will find in other commentaries; they should read Aristotle's text and decide for themselves who is right in their understanding of it. Most conspicuously, the doctrine of the mean has been interpreted as being a doctrine of moderation – the thesis that extremes are to be avoided and that the middle way is the safest.

Unless Aristotle is guilty of a very serious mistake, basic and not in detail, this interpretation must be totally wrong. For Aristotle, as he repeatedly makes clear, excellence of character is a willingness to act in whatever way practical reason requires, and the doctrine of the mean is part of Aristotle's formal definition of excellence of character. But the doctrine of moderation, however interpreted in detail, is clearly a principle determining what action is appropriate on each occasion; as such, it is clearly, if correct, a deliverance of practical thinking and not an attribute of character. Thus, if the doctrine of the mean were a thesis of moderation, it would be guilty of confusing excellence of character with that practical wisdom which, Aristotle repeatedly says, must guide our deliberations and our actions.

Moreover, the doctrine of moderation, while reasonable enough at a crude practical level (like 'keep your cool' or 'don't fly off the handle'), if not taken literally, is hard to interpret to make philosophical sense. Surely we are not supposed to exhibit a moderate amount of fear, anger and every other emotion whenever we act? Clearly the right amount of most emotions to display on most occasions is zero. Does it, then, say that when a display of anger is appropriate we should always be moderately angry? But the suggestion that we should be moderately angry when faced with a trivial slight and when witnessing wanton cruelty is absurd; there are occasions on which we cannot be too angry, just as there are occasions when, at most, a slight degree of annoyance is in order.

So the thesis of moderation, or any other account of the doctrine of the mean that makes it a device for deciding how to act, can have nothing to do with the Aristotelian view put forward in the *Ethics*. We must look for another interpretation, which is not hard to find if we take Aristotle to mean what he says.

The doctrine of the mean is part of the definition of excellence of character. Though Aristotle holds that the aim of his ethical work is practical and not to discover what excellence of character is (1108b 27), he clearly thinks that theoretical understanding contributes to that practical end, for in Chapter 5 of Book II he raises the question 'What is excellence of character?'. This is the regular formula for a demand for a definition of the Aristotelian type. A definition of this type should be constructed by first determining the genus of the thing to be defined, or, less technically, by determining to what wide class of things it belongs and then determining its specific difference, or, less technically, by determining how what is to be defined differs from everything else in the genus. Thus the famous Aristotelian definition of man as a rational animal places man in the genus *animal* and then differentiates him from all other sorts of animal by his rationality. We shall find that Aristotle gives a definition of excellence of character strictly in accordance with this theory.

Having asked the question what excellence of character is, Aristotle has little difficulty in showing that it is a disposition or settled state. Moreover in Chapter 5 he has told us that it is a settled disposition with regard to the feeling and displaying of emotions. Any action that displays character at all, he holds, will involve the display of some emotion, such as 'desire, anger, fear, confidence, envy, joy, friendliness, hatred, longing, emulation, pity' (1105b 20–21); no doubt he would agree that actions undertaken as part of a long chain of means will often display emotion only indirectly, but there must always be the basic emotional drive. Anger, or any other emotion, is not in itself either an excellence or a defect of character, but a settled state with regard to exhibiting it will be an excellence if it is a disposition to act in a way directed by sound practical wisdom, a defect if it is a disposition towards improper action. The states of character are distinguished as being specific excellences or defects according to the emotion involved: bravery and cowardice are an excellence and a defect displayed in relation to the emotion fear, even and hot temper are so related to anger, temperance and gluttony to appetite for food, and so on. Excellences and defects are distinguished by the emotions they display.

'So we have stated to what genus excellence of character belongs' (1106a 13); it is a settled state or disposition. But there are many settled states, and not a few settled states of character with regard to the emotions, of which excellence of character is only one. So, not surprisingly, Aristotle immediately recognizes that he must go on to say how excellence of character differs from other states of character. 'But we must not merely say that it is a disposition, but also what sort of disposition' (1106b 14–15); Aristotle must complete the definition by stating the difference. The doctrine of the mean provides this completion.

It will be helpful if we know in advance what other states of character Aristotle recognizes; if he were to recognize only one – badness of character – it could be very simply distinguished from excellence; but in fact he recognizes many more. Unfortunately, Aristotle has not yet mentioned any of these other states of character except in passing, which is perhaps a defect in his order of exposition. But he does give a list at the beginning of Book VII, where he distinguishes six states, divisible into three contrary pairs. One of the pairs is formed by, on the one hand, a super-human excellence which might be called heroic, and is attributable only to the gods; its contrary is a sub-human beastliness indicative of disease or madness – the sort of state which in modern times might lead to the criminal lunatic asylum rather than the prison. As super-human and sub-human, these are perhaps not really states of human character at all, and I shall say no more about them. Aristotle himself says very little about these conditions. Another of these contrary pairs is excellence of character and badness of character. But there is also a third pair of contraries, one of which might be called strength of will or self-control, the other weakness of will or lack of self-control. These states characterize the man who needs and tries to make himself act properly, unlike the man of excellent character who acts properly without any difficulty; the one who succeeds in making himself so act is the strong-willed man, and the one who tries and fails is weak willed.

Thus, if we may neglect the super- and sub-human in studying human excellence, we have four states of character that need to be distinguished from one other. In order of decreasing merit, they are:

(1) Excellence of character: the state of the man who wants to act appropriately and does so without internal friction.
(2) Strength of will: the state of the man who wants to act improperly but makes himself act properly.

(3) Weakness of will: the state of the man who wants to act improperly, tries to make himself act properly, and fails.

(4) Badness of character: the state of the man who wants to act improperly, who thinks it an excellent idea so to do, and does so without internal friction.

We can illustrate the situation with a sort of table:

	Want	*Aim*	*Act*
Excellence	Good	Good	Good
Strength	Bad	Good	Good
Weakness	Bad	Good	Bad
Badness	Bad	Bad	Bad

Thus these four states can be distinguished from each other in so far as no two display the same merit in both the emotional want, the aim or choice settled on after deliberation, and in action. The four states could get a modern illustration from the even-tempered man who has no difficulty in waiting coolly in a traffic jam, the hot-tempered man who successfully restrains himself, the hot-tempered man who tries to remain calm but cannot and the man who curses and hoots at all and sundry with complete self-approval.

So it appears that Aristotle thinks that no emotion is, in itself, either good or bad; what is good or bad is a disposition to display emotions appropriately or inappropriately. It would be foreign to Aristotle's teleological view of nature to allow that we are naturally endowed with emotions that should never be exhibited or felt. What we still need is some further clarification of the notion of propriety, and that is what Aristotle gives us in the doctrine of the mean. Aristotle holds that excellence of character is a disposition to feel and display the right degree of emotion on each occasion and as the occasion demands, and that this disposition is in a mean between being too much disposed and too little disposed to feel and display each emotion. In the mean one will feel and display each emotion at the right times and not too often or too infrequently, with reference to the right matters, towards the right people, for the right reason and in the right way. To be inclined to excess will involve such errors as feeling and displaying an emotion in season and out of season, in inappropriate situations, towards people indiscriminately, without good cause and in inappropriate ways. A similar account can be given of being inclined to deficiency.

The abbreviated account of excess and deficiency is simply 'too much' and 'too little'; it is this that has most probably led readers to interpret the doctrine as one of moderation, a view that one must avoid extremes of emotion and action on every occasion. But plenty of passages prove this to be a mistake. Here is one: 'Fear and confidence and appetite and anger and pity and in general likes and dislikes may be felt both too much and too little, and in both cases not well; but to feel them at the right time, with reference to the right objects, towards the right people, with the right motive, and in the right way, is what is both intermediate and best, and this is characteristic of excellence' (1106b 19–23).

Thus there will be, in the traditional terminology, two vices correlated with each virtue, or two types of bad character correlated with each excellence of character, not just one. Aristotle does not think we should accept this just on the basis of the general considerations so far adduced, but should consider the individual excellences and see whether we can find two defects going with each excellence (1107a 28–29). In the *Nicomachean Ethics* he refers us to a table that is missing from the text (1107a 33) but does discuss briefly a few cases. However, a fairly long list is given in the *Eudemian Ethics*, which is reproduced here for convenience:

Irascibility	impassivity	even temper
foolhardiness	cowardice	bravery
shamelessness	touchiness	modesty
intemperance	insensibility	temperance
envy	(nameless)	fair-mindedness
gain	disadvantage	justice
prodigality	meanness	liberality
boastfulness	mock modesty	truthfulness
flattery	churlishness	friendliness

servility	disdain	dignity
vanity	mean spirit	pride
ostentation	unworldliness	magnificence

Not all these examples will be convincing to the modern reader without more ado, but they illustrate the general contention.

We should note, to dispel the ghost of moderation, that excellence of character is explicitly said to be an intermediate disposition towards action (1106b 31) and not a disposition to intermediate action. Extreme action will on some occasions be appropriate and carried out by the man of excellent character. Thus the man whose temper is good will be mildly angry about trifles and enraged by outrages, whereas the irascible man will be excessively angry over trifles and the placid or impassive man may be little or only moderately angered by the worst excesses. To give another modern example: the hot-tempered man will also be liable to rage at the helpless telephonist as well as at the person responsible for letting him down, while the over-placid man will just shrug his shoulders. These are illustrations of the many ways in which both excess and deficiency can be exhibited. Simply being too angry or not angry enough on a given occasion are only one way in which excess and deficiency can be exhibited.

It is commonly said that the doctrine of the mean argues that to every virtue there correspond two vices. But, whereas some of the states of character exhibiting excess or defect might be reasonably, if somewhat archaically, called vices, such as intemperance, others could not; some, while flaws in a person's make-up, are barely, if at all, of moral significance. No doubt a person is to some degree badly adjusted if he has no enjoyment in even the simple food necessary for health, of if he is overplacid in temperament, or is too self-effacing; but these are not vices nor even moral misdemeanours. Aristotle is considering that states of character do or do not conduce to the *eudaemon* life, whereas to call a character trait a vice is, in modern English, a moral condemnation. We must also be careful about our understanding of the expressions 'bad character' and 'good character'. For Aristotle, a bad character is one which detracts from eudaemonia, not because he has no conception of or no interest in wrong-doing, but because wrong-doing is not what he is at this stage concerned to discuss.

So Aristotle can arrive at his final definition of excellences of character. 'It is a settled state of choice, in a mean relative to us, which mean is determined by reason as the wise man determines it' (1106b 36–1107a 2). The notion of choice and the part played by reason will, of course, require further elucidation, by Aristotle and in this book. By saying that the mean is relative to us Aristotle is making it clear that he is not using any mathematical notion, such as those of an arithmetical or geometrical mean, but that the mean is determined by, is relative to, all the circumstances in which the choice of actions has to be made.

The statement that excellence of character is in a mean and that this serves to differentiate it from other human dispositions and settled states perhaps requires some justification. To say that excellence of character is in a mean is to say that the emotions that are its domain can be experienced and displayed in action both too much and too little. Let us, anticipating a little our discussion of theoretical excellence, contrast excellence of character with one excellence of theoretical intelligence which Aristotle tells us is concerned with grasping basic truths. But there is no possibility of grasping basic truths too much, too frequently, etcetera; there is only one fault corresponding to the excellence – intellectual dullness, inability to grasp these truths.

In this way, and because, also, excellence of character is the only human disposition concerned with choice at all, the thesis that it is differentiated by choice in a mean, can serve to differentiate excellence of character from other human excellences. Aristotle, of course, realizes, and indeed claims, that intermediates can often be best in other areas. Thus, in relation to health, one can take too much or too little exercise and eat too much or too little food. Here, too, the mean is relative to us, since different people with different occupations will need different quantities and types of food and exercise. Aristotle does not need to claim that only the thing defined exhibits the specific difference;he needs to claim only that it is the one thing within the genus that exhibits the feature. Similarly, God is rational, but Aristotle can define man as a rational animal since God is not an animal. His claim is that exhibiting mean choice applies only to those settled human dispositions that are excellences of character, and that it characterizes all of these.

We have seen that the whole of this account of excellence of character, including the doctrine of the mean, is theoretical, not practical, since it has been devoted to the discovery of a definition. Its theoretical character becomes more obvious by contrast with the very end of Book II, where Aristotle does offer some directly practical advice. There he notes that it is not easy to be sure what action will on each occasion exhibit a mean disposition, so that when in doubt one should veer towards the extreme which is less pernicious than the other and also away from the one that one is more inclined to lean towards. If, for example, one were inclined to be too meek, one should, when in doubt, aim towards the side of self-assertiveness, while, if being too angry were worse than not being as angry as the occasion warrants, one should, for that reason also, tend towards mildness. Aristotle also notes that one cannot in practical matters ever determine exactly where the mean lies and how far one has to depart from it before one is deserving of blame, nor can one lay down precise rules for determining the mean. 'The decision rests with perception' says Aristotle (1109b 23), by which laconic remark he does not mean that one sees, intuits, in some ineffable way how to behave, but that you need to be present in the particular situation to judge, and no general principle can be comprehensive enough to take account of the values of all the variables to be taken account of. In the same way, he notes, only the man on the spot can decide whether the bread is properly cooked (1113a 1).

This whole approach to the problems of action is in striking contrast to such modern ethical doctrines as regard certain kinds of action as invariably right in themselves and others as invariably wrong; Kant claimed, for example, that lying, promise breaking and suicide were of their own nature wrong. Others would claim that some emotions are in themselves evil and a mark of the depravity of human nature. But Aristotle is aware of the possibility of such views, and explains that the difference between them and his is more apparent than real. Thus, he agrees that the emotional state called shamelessness is in itself always and inevitably bad (1107a 11): but this is because shamelessness is the name given to an emotion only when in excess, the same emotion being called modesty when in a mean. 'Some things are named with their worthlessness included' (1107a 10), but these are already extremes. Such principles as 'Never display excess or deficiency of an emotion' are, no doubt, true, but are empty. In the same way, some actions are always wrong, such as adultery and murder, which are named with their worthlessness included. But adultery will usually be a manifestation of excessive sexual desire, excessive in this case because towards the wrong person; homicide, similarly, is only called murder when unjustified. Murder will frequently exhibit an excess of anger or greed. Aristotle is clearly to some degree successful in dealing with these apparent exceptions to his view. But there do remain disagreements with such views as those of Kant, for it is not clear how Aristotle could claim that lying and suicide, for example, could be defined in an evaluative way which made their condemnation universal but empty.

Finally, here is a summary of the main points of Aristotle's account of excellence of character:

1   All action directly or indirectly exhibits some emotion.
2   For each specific excellence of character there will be some specific emotion whose field it is.
3   In the case of each such emotion it is possible to be disposed to exhibit it to the right degree; this is excellence of character.
4   In the case of each such emotion it is possible to be disposed to exhibit it too much or too little, and each of these dispositions is a defect of character.
5   'Too much' includes 'on too many occasions' and similar possibilities as well as 'too violently'; 'too little' includes 'on too few occasions' and similar possibilities as well as 'too weakly'.
6   The right amount has to be determined by reason.
7   So excellence can be defined as being a settled disposition of choice in a mean relative to us, such as the wise man would determine it.
8   There is no emotion that no one should ever exhibit.

3

Action and its Motives

The attentive reader will have noticed two elements in the discussion of excellence of character that may well have proved puzzling; they are the intimate link presumed to exist between emotion and action and also between emotion and our likes and dislikes, or, in other words, what gives us pleasure and what distresses us. In order to understand these and connected matters we need to go back to what, in Aristotle's view, are questions prior to ethics, and particularly to matters discussed in Book II of his *On the Soul (De Anima)*.

All organisms, Aristotle held, have two primary needs, without which the species could not survive, to maintain their own lives and to reproduce themselves. Towards this end, he thought, plants had no need of sensation, emotion, desires, or motion from place to place. Being rooted in the ground, they obtained the nourishment they needed automatically and without any activity or effort on their part; they needed no eyes to locate their food and no movement to ingest it. Their mode of reproduction was equally passive so far as they were concerned, however important the activity of bees and the wind. But an animal that remained immobile could neither maintain its own life nor reproduce itself. But now the question arises why an animal should maintain its own life and why it should not just allow itself to perish. The answer that Aristotle gave is that an animal has sensations and emotions, and that these are inherently either pleasant or distressing; to find something pleasant is one and the same thing as to desire it and to find it distressing is to desire to avoid it. Leaving aside unreal and apparent exceptions, such as masochism, the notion of finding something both distressing and desirable is incoherent.

Animals are so constituted as to find pleasant that which tends towards their own preservation and to the reproduction of their species, most obviously eating, drinking and sexual activity, and find the lack of these, hunger, thirst and sexual deprivation, distressing. So animals move, eat, drink, copulate, and generally behave as they do behave, in order to obtain what they like, what gives them pleasure, and to avoid what they dislike, what distresses them.

It is important to be aware that this sort of desire, which Ross always calls 'appetite' in his translation, is, as a matter of definition, for the pleasant and to avoid the unpleasant. Pleasure simply is that which is the object of appetite; appetite is what leads animals to behave as they do, and one of the things that lead men, who are also animals, to behave as they do.

For Aristotle, what I have called 'emotion' and in standard translations is called 'passion', essentially includes likes and dislikes, pleasure and distress, and hence appetite and hence action. Thus, fear essentially includes a desire for avoidance and for safety; it is hard to see how a person could be genuinely afraid of something and yet have no tendency to attempt to avoid it. In his *Rhetoric* Aristotle defines anger as a desire, accompanied by distress, for a real or apparent revenge, and the discussion of anger in Book IV, Chapter 5 of the *Nicomachean Ethics* shows no change of mind. Pity includes a desire to relieve distress. At 1105b 21 he gives a list of emotions relevant to excellence of character and adds: 'and in general that on which pleasure or distress is consequent'. But where there is pleasure or distress, there will be appetite to gain or avoid, and hence a tendency to action. The reader may or may not think that the word 'emotion' or the word 'passion' marks a concept which is so closely linked to that of action; but there is no doubt that Aristotle sees the close link in the concept which these translations, however imperfect, seek to refer to.

For Aristotle, man is an animal which shares these emotions and appetites with other animals; for him, man differs from other animals by having something they have not, but not lacking anything that they have. Man is rational, and this enables him to have another kind of desire which, following Ross's regular practice, I shall call 'rational wish', or simply 'wish'. Just as appetite is, by definition, for the pleasant, so rational wish is for the good.

It is clear that to satisfy one's immediate desires can be disadvantageous and even ruinous. Appetite can lead mice into traps and men into alcoholism, drug addiction, venereal disease, and many lesser disasters. An animal, such as man, needs to have foresight, a knowledge of general natural regularities, memory and the power of planning and deliberation, if he is to be able to forgo satisfaction of immediate appetite and aim for long-term satisfaction, for the good and ultimately for eudaemonia. According to Aristotle, man alone has these rational powers and so has rational wishes, as well as appetites; this may be unjust to animals, but that issue is not now relevant.

Rational wish for the good must not be misunderstood as meaning something like desire for the morally right or the general welfare; basically, it means something like desire for what on the basis of rational calculation is seen to serve one's best interest in the long run. This is true though, as we have already seen, such rational deliberation is thought by Aristotle to prompt us to acquire and maintain excellence of character as being of value to us, and therefore to be just, honest, truthful and so on. Rational wish on the basis of sound deliberation is opposed to the selfishness into which our unguided appetites might lead us.

Since the ultimate end is eudaemonia, Aristotle has no doubt that when rational wish contradicts appetite it is desirable that rational wish should prevail. But the appetites are an essential ingredient in human nature and should be guided, not supplanted, by reason. Reason on its own is inert (1139a 36); one could not be either prudent or imprudent in one's eating habits without the basic need and desire for food, one could exhibit no excellence of character if there were no emotion, and hence appetite, to be guided by practical wisdom. The interplay between appetite and reason, that alone makes rational wish possible, is a central theme of Aristotle's Ethics; without both of them there could be no characteristically human action.

We have so far distinguished two species of the genus desire, appetite and rational wish. For the sake of completeness and accuracy it must be added that Aristotle recognized a third species of human desire that he calls (in Greek) *thumos*. I leave the term untranslated because I am not sure what the best translation would be, since I do not understand the role of *thumos*. The term has been variously translated as 'anger', 'spirit', 'self-respect', and that is not a complete list.

Readers of Plato's *Republic* will remember that there Plato distinguishes three elements in the tripartite soul, the rational element (which seems to correspond roughly to Aristotle's rational wish and which aims at the good), appetite, as in Aristotle's threefold classification of desires, and *thumos*. *Thumos* is said to characterize the military type of men who form the middle class, or caste, in his ideal state. Aristotle appears to have taken over the threefold classification from the *Republic*. This threefold distinction is found for the first time in the *Nicomachean Ethics* at 1111b 11, where it is mentioned quite casually and without any explanation. It is discussed at 1116b 23ff and at 1149a 26ff. It appears to characterize mainly the soldier and generally the brave. Perhaps it corresponds somewhat to that sense of honour that the military used to be so touchy about. What is puzzling is why it should figure alongside rational wish and appetite as a further fundamental type of desire. Luckily, the notion of *thumos* plays a very slight and unimportant role in Aristotle's general ethical theory.

4

Responsibility and Choice

At the beginning of Chapter 7 of Book II Aristotle has said that his general theory of excellence of character must be tested by examining particular excellences to make sure that they fit into the general characterization, and he immediately makes a very abbreviated examination of some of them. Before he goes on to examine the particular excellences in more detail, he discusses, in the first part of Book III, some general questions about the general nature of action, with particular reference to questions of responsibility for action and, hence, liability to praise and blame. He first discusses under what circumstances one can be absolved of responsibility, on the assumption that we are normally responsible for what we do; afterwards he examines the ground for that assumption.

We must first note a tiresome point of translation. I shall use the terms 'intended', 'contrary to intention' and 'unintended' as the names of three classes of action distinguished by Aristotle. Ross's translation has 'voluntary' instead of 'intended', 'involuntary' instead of 'contrary to intention' and 'not voluntary' instead of 'unintended', as do some others; sometimes translators have 'willing' instead of 'intended' and 'unwilling' instead of 'contrary to intention'; this is a confusing nuisance for the Greekless reader. No translation sounds invariably idiomatic in English, but I think the one I have chosen best reflects the sense of the original. We speak of involuntary cries and grimaces, for example, but these are not the sort of thing that Aristotle has primarily in mind; he is thinking of such things as misleading others because one is oneself misinformed, which is more reasonably called contrary to intention than involuntary or unwilling. Or again we shall find that Aristotle holds that when we act reluctantly under pressure we are still liable to praise and blame, but it would be odd to say that we did so willingly, reasonable to say that it was a case of intentional though unwilling action.

Good and bad characters are liable to praise and blame, and so are the actions that flow from them. We must, therefore, Aristotle holds, consider which actions are relevant for determining character, since we are liable to praise and blame for only some of our actions. The discussion of these matters is terse, meaty, important in itself and very relevant to questions of jurisprudence and to problems of punishment. But it is easily misunderstood, so we must examine it with care.

Aristotle starts his discussion by saying that people are praised and blamed for intended actions, but that they receive pardon or pity for what they do contrary to intention. This he states as an obvious truth that requires no argument to justify it.

When, then, is an action contrary to intention? Aristotle's answer is that there are two fundamentally different types of case, one involving force and one ignorance. He deals first with force (1110a 1ff). He makes it clear that he is referring to actual physical force exerted on the person in question, whether it be applied by men or by nature, not such things as pressure of circumstances. If one is supposed to go, and fully intends to go, to Athens but ends up in Smyrna, because one is kidnapped and taken to Smyrna, or because gales blow one's ship off course to Smyrna, then one's arrival in Smyrna is obviously contrary to intention and nobody would assign any blame. Correctly translated at 1110a 2–3, which is not always the case, Aristotle notes that this sort of affair is not really an action at all but simply something that happens to one: the agency is from outside, he says, and 'nothing is contributed by the agent or, rather, the person it happens to'.

Aristotle has nothing more to say about this case, which is obviously quite straightforward. But he notes that it is important to distinguish it from another sort of case, where we might speak of a person as acting under compulsion, but where actual physical force which he is powerless to resist is not the question. He tells us what sort of cases he has in mind — for example, when we do something discreditable on the command of a tyrant who has our family in his power and threatens to kill them unless we obey him, a spectacular case of blackmail, or when a ship's captain throws his cargo overboard in a storm to save his ship from sinking and his crew from drowning.

Certainly in such cases we may say that we were compelled to do what we did and that we did not want to do it. But Aristotle rightly points out that in such cases our action was intended at the time it took place, even though in the abstract it was contrary to intention. To put this in other words, if the captain were asked whether he intended at that time to save his ship and crew by jettisoning his cargo, his true answer would be that he did; if asked simply whether it was his intention to dump his cargo, without reference to circumstances, he would justifiably reply that it was not. Such actions Aristotle calls mixed (1110a 11) since these two answers are possible.

We may bring out the difference in these two types of cases by noting that when irresistible physical force is applied we can deny that we can be properly described as doing the action at all — 'I didn't really barge into you, I was pushed'. In the other sort of case we admit that we performed the action, but we either justify it, like the sea captain in our illustration in which case, as Aristotle says (1110a 20), we may well be praised for our action, or we palliate it with the result that we are pardoned, as also in cases where human nature is overstretched and nobody would be able to resist, such as severe torture (1110a 24–25). But there is also the unpardonable, Aristotle thinks, that can never be an acceptable way out of a bad situation, for example, matricide; one should rather die, having suffered the worst tortures, than do such a deed. Perhaps Aristotle, excusably, has not allowed for the most diabolical modern police methods; perhaps there are cases where ingenious physical and psychological techniques remove the sufferer's responsibility so that what he does cannot be considered an action at all. Perhaps then the case can be assimilated to those where irresistable physical force is involved and there is no agency. But there remains an important difference between cases where an accused person pleads that he did not do that of which he is accused and those where the accused admits the action but attempts to justify it or at least to excuse or palliate it. We have here two fundamentally different ways of escaping blame. In the one case the accused can claim that since he did not do the alleged deed he cannot be blamed for it; in the other case the accused accepts responsibility but claims that the circumstances obviate or reduce blame. In the first case the position is much the same as if the accused were to present an alibi, save that, instead of denying his bodily presence, the accused claims that the event was something that merely happened to his body; the deed was not his.

We may just mention a short sarcastic note by Aristotle on those who attempt to escape responsibility by saying that they were forced by their desires (1110b 9ff). Aristotle makes two quick points: first, that acting in accordance with desire is the paradigm case of acting responsibly, second, that it is always their bad deeds that people attempt to disclaim in this way, never their good deeds. Nobody says that we should not praise saints and heroes, on the ground that, products of their environment, they cannot help it. This debate, as we know, continues today.

We have now examined one of the two types of situation which Aristotle believes exonerate the person principally involved of responsibility and most recently, the case of 'mixed actions' which need to be distinguished from cases of brute force.

The other type of case is one in which the agent is ignorant of facts, which, had he known them, would have led him to act otherwise. Aristotle commences this discussion by making a very good distinction between what is merely unintended and what is contrary to intention (1110b 18ff). Clearly, if a person's act has a feature which he had not foreseen and of which, when acting, he was unaware, that person could not have intended it to have that feature. But there are always many features of everything that one does of which one is ignorant and about which one is totally indifferent. Thus, when one puts on a shoe, one is probably unaware that it weighs just so much, was made by such and such a person, in such and such a place, and so on. But it is very unlikely that it would be contary to one's intention to put on a shoe with such a history; if one had known all these facts it usually would not have made the slightest difference.

Aristotle's view, obviously correct, is that the mere fact that a feature of one's act was unknown to one, and is therefore unintended, does not remove responsibility. Responsibility is lessened or removed only if the feature unknown was contrary to one's intention, so that, if one had known, one would not have done the deed. Aristotle is sometimes criticized for giving as the criterion for an action's being not merely unintended but contrary to intention that it is distressing and regretted or, in Ross's translation, that it 'produces pain and regret' (1110b 19). It is objected that subsequent regret, remorse, repentance, grief, cannot alter the nature of the act at the time of performance, while at the time of action the agent is unaware of what he is doing so cannot then regret it. This is perfectly true, but is not a valid objection, since it is a misunderstanding of the point at issue. Aristotle surely means that the criterion of whether at the time of the action the ignorance was material or irrelevant is whether one would have acted otherwise if one had known the facts in question. The obvious test of whether one would have acted differently is whether one does regret the deed and say: 'If only I had known', when the ignorance is removed. It is this sort of regret and not later repentence that is relevant. There is nothing at the time of action by which one could distinguish between what is merely unintended and what is contrary to intention. Whether one would have acted differently had one known, the best, though not conclusive, evidence for this is the response one makes when the ignorance is removed. There is nothing very subtle about this; if I knock into you in the street and then say I am sorry, you will take it that the contact was contrary to my intention; people who do not care whether they barge into other people or not are not sorry when they do.

It must be emphasized that one escapes blame by pleading ignorance only when it is a case of acting, in Aristotle's words 'through ignorance of particular facts' (1110b 33). This is contrasted with two types of case of not knowing how to behave, the drunken person who, while drunk, thinks it rather witty to throw away empty glasses and break windows, and the man of bad character. Both are examples of not knowing how to behave, and Aristotle thinks this sort of ignorance to be no excuse (1110b 25–32). This may not chime with some modern views, by which not knowing how to behave is ascribed to heredity and environment and excused, and badness, if acknowledged at all, is thought to be the transgressing of principles one does know, when one 'knows better'. But Aristotle, as we have already noted and shall document later in detail, distinguishes weakness of will, or lack of self-control, from badness of character. The gratuitous violence of those who think it good sport to rough people up is what Aristotle has in mind as an example of bad character, and their ignorance consists in their thinking it a good idea; the violence of the man who knows it to be wrong but fails to control his temper is a different matter, though still a fault.

It may well seem to the reader that Aristotle's account of the circumstances in which blame can be avoided, admitting only force and ignorance of particular fact, is too narrow. If one were to interpret 'ignorance of fact' in a narrow sense this criticism would be justified. But when Aristotle gives a series of illustrations of what he has in mind when speaking of ignorance of fact it becomes clear that we have to interpret the phrase 'ignorance of fact' in a very wide sense. These illustrations are given, in a very laconic and sometimes rather baffling way, at 1111a 10–20. No doubt Aeschylus' defence, when he was charged with revealing the rites of the ceremony of initiation into the Mysteries, that he did not know it to be forbidden, is a straightforward case of pleading ignorance of a piece of information. But when Merope killed her son, thinking him to be an enemy, this seems to be a case of failure of recognition or of mistaken identity; she misinterpreted the facts rather than being ignorant of them, though she could say 'I did not know that it was my son'. Again, if one is intending merely to show somebody a catapult but lets it off (presumably thereby causing injury, though Aristotle does not develop the illustration), this is surely a case of clumsiness, or an accident, or inadvertence, though one could say 'I did not know it would go off'. Again, if one hits a sparring partner too hard, it seems to be an accident or error of judgement rather than ignorance of the situation in which one was acting. It is clear that Aristotle is using the expression 'ignorance of fact' to cover all these cases. The crucial test seems to be whether one foresaw at the time of acting that the action would fall under the relevant description. Merope did not know that hers would fall under the description 'she killed her son', the man with the catapult did not know that his action would fall under the description 'he shot his friend with a catapult'. Aeschylus did not know that he was revealing a secret, and so on. When this is seen, the charge that 'ignorance of fact' is too narrow is at least somewhat blunted. But when we remember that this is, so far as is known, the first attempt ever to set out systematically the principles involved in assigning responsibility, praise and blame, we must admit that it is a remarkably good one.

We should note the point of view from which Aristotle has discussed these issues. It is clear that he is looking at them from a rather forensic point of view. He is asking under what circumstances one can avoid responsibility for an action under some particular description, not asking how the action, considered from all points of view, reflects on the agent's character. Thus, if one believes that some liquid is an appropriate medicine to give to an ailing friend and it turns out to be a poison that kills him, Aristotle is concerned to point out that one may escape blame for the death, not to emphasize that the action displays a caring disposition, though he shows that he is not unaware of this aspect of the situation (1110a 23–24). This is not a defect of his treatment, since he is in the relevant passages discussing under what circumstances responsibility can be successfully repudiated; but it should be noted that this is his approach.

Finally, on this topic, we may ask when ignorance of the facts is an excuse. Should one not make sure that the liquid is medicine and not poison, that the spear is not sharpened and that the catapult is handled safely? Aristotle does not consider this point in detail. He does point out that if blinded by drink or rage the culprit cannot escape blame (1110b 25–30) and at 1113b 30 he says positively that the drunken agent is responsible because he made himself drunk. Clearly a more through examination of the question of justified and unjustified ignorance would be possible. The reader may care to look forward to Chapter 8 of Book V, where some relevant issues are raised and Aristotle makes a distinction between bad luck, which is the situation when things turn out in a way that could not be reasonably expected, and mistakes which are made when events are not so unforeseeable.

CHOICE

Aristotle begins the second chapter of Book III with the statement that now the intended and unintended have been distinguished 'we must discuss choice'. It is not clear why this particular order is thought proper, but the sequence is reasonable; we are still involved in an examination of the main features of action that reflect on character and, as Aristotle says, chosen actions are a subdivision of those intended. Thus the discussion of choice 'is closely related to excellence, and better indicates character than action does' (1111b 5–6). All chosen actions are intended, but not all intended actions are chosen.

Small children and animals, like grown-up people, act intentionally, according to Aristotle. Some commentators, including those who disapprove of the translation 'intention', deny this. But Aristotle, in *On the Motion of Animals (De Motu Animalium)*, where he gives his theory to explain how animals come to act, gives a teleological explanation of how animals come to act through appetite (it must be remembered that Aristotle believes that there are many complementary types of explanation, and the teleological does not exclude others). Aristotle is surely right on the main issue; there is all the difference in the world between, say an intended kick by a horse and accidental contact with its hoof. But even if we neglect this point, it is clear that some actions of adult human beings are intended but not chosen, such as those done on the spur of the moment (1111b 9–11).

What, then, is choice? Aristotle has distinguished three types of motivation, appetite, spirit, and rational wish, so if choice leads to action it must be distinguished from these.

Choice is not the same as appetite or spirit, because choice involves the use of reason. Moreover, choice must be distinct from appetite since the two may easily conflict. It is the mark of the weak-willed man that he acts in accordance with his appetite and contrary to his considered choice, while the strong-willed man succeeds in conquering his appetite and acts as he has chosen; the man of good character does not, as we have seen, suffer this conflict. Readers should be warned against misunderstanding such translations as those of Ross: 'The incontinent man acts with appetite, but not with choice; while the continent man on the contrary acts with choice, but not appetite' (1111b 13–15). This must not be taken to mean that weak-willed (incontinent) men make no choices and strong-willed (continent) men have no appetites. If strong-willed men had no appetites then, to talk Irish, they would not need to be strong-willed.

So of the three basic types of motivation, appetite, spirit (anger) and rational wish, appetite has been eliminated from being identical with choice. Aristotle dismisses spirit, or anger, as obviously wrong (1111b 18). But rational wish seems to be a more promising candidate since it, like choice, involves the use of reason. However Aristotle now makes the point that they cannot be the same since one can rationally wish for all kinds of things that one knows to be impossible, such as to live for ever or be twenty feet tall; but one can choose only among realistic possibilities. One cannot choose to go on living indefinitely.

We should note that Aristotle is here making a conceptual point that will be important more than once in his ethical discussions. He is not talking about what it is psychologically possible for human beings to achieve, for example. He does not think that a person who chose to do what he knew to be impossible would be overambitious, or stupid, or even plain crazy. Aristotle says that anyone who *said* that he chose to do the impossible would have to be crazy (1111b 20–22). 'I wish to go on living for ever, though I know that I cannot' makes good sense linguistically, however foolish in content; 'I choose to live for ever though I know I cannot' could be said only by someone ignorant of the meaning of the words he uses.

Aristotle also makes the further conceptual point that just as one cannot choose to do the impossible, so one can choose to do only what is in one's power and does not depend on others. Thus, one can choose to apply for a job, but cannot choose to obtain it. This is manifestly one of the points that needs to be understood sympathetically.No doubt one could be prevented from applying for a job by kidnappers, for example; but in saying 'I choose' one implicitly rules such possibilities out of consideration.

Aristotle gives an explanation of these points which, since it is of a conceptual matter, itself involves conceptual distinctions. There are many concepts which contain within them the implication of success. Thus to win (a battle or a race) is to compete successfully, to be healthy is to succeed in being in good bodily condition, and to live the good life, to be *eudaemon,* is to live one's whole life successfully. One can wish for any sort of success, but choice is not to succeed but to do whatever is necessary for success. It does not make sense, Aristotle says, to talk of choosing to succeed, of choosing to be healthy, for example (1111b 29). On this point Aristotle is surely right. One can talk of choosing to succeed only in a secondary sense. No doubt one can 'choose' to win or lose a 'race' with a small child; but in this secondary sense to lose will be as much a success as to win or, more accurately, to win as little a success as to lose.

This is, no doubt, a conceptual distinction taken from common discourse, employing the common-sense notion of what is in our power and what is not. The sceptical, or ultracautious, philosopher will tell us that no overt action is within our power; even moving our finger depends on our nerves and muscles functioning as we expect them to and a host of other favourable circumstances; a paralysed man cannot choose to move his finger. If faced by such a philosopher Aristotle would, I think, remind him of the point made at the beginning of the *Nicomachean Ethics* that one should expect a degree of accuracy appropriate to one's subject matter. At the level of ethics the distinction between what is in our power and what is not and the distinction between what we can do unaided and what we can do only with the cooperation of others are both acceptable, however close a scrutiny they may require in the philosophy of action.

We have been speaking in terms of success, such as winning or proving, for which we may wish, however unlikely or even impossible it may be, and what is necessary for success, as competing is necessary if one is to win and arguing if one is to prove. What we thus do must be in our power if we are to choose to do it. The terminology used for making this distinction is usually that of calling the success 'the end' and what we choose in order to achieve success 'the means'. Aristotle's own words for what is thus called 'the means' are: 'the things towards the end (goal, success, terminal point)' (1111b 26, 1112b 12, etc.). In a normal sense, 'means to the end' is far too restrictive. Thus, if the end, goal, success for which one wishes is to win a race, then the means that one might choose to take towards that end might include certain exercise and diet; but running the race would not normally be called a means towards winning. Yet running the race is something in our power that we can choose. More importantly, working out what, on a given occasion, would constitute excellence in action would not naturally be called choosing a means, but it is for Aristotle one of the most important types of choice that we have to make. So we must constantly be aware that wish is for success and that choice is concerned as much with determining what course of action will be the successful one as with determining the means towards the chosen course of action.

So choice is not to be identified with appetite, spirit (anger) or wish, though it would have no function without wish. If one had no wishes one could not plan and choose the best way to achieve them. But choice must also be distinguished from belief (1111b 30 ff). Obviously it cannot be identified with belief in general, since some beliefs, such as those about mathematics, have no practical relevance. But Aristotle makes the important point that choice of the best is to be distinguished from belief about what is best; our choice determines our character, not our beliefs, and we can have beliefs about what is good for others, but can choose only for ourselves. No doubt belief influences our choices and our actions, but it cannot be identified with either.

Aristotle's tentative conclusion is that choice is that which is intended as the result of deliberation (1112a 15–16). Thus it is clear that our regular translation 'choice' does not quite capture Aristotle's thought. We can, for example, speak of making a random choice, where there is no deliberation, and the word 'choice' suggests selection from a range of possibilities already before us. Perhaps some other translation might be better, such as 'decision'. In any case, we know that what Aristotle is discussing is the determination of what to do in order to achieve what we wish for, and that we wish for what seems to us to be best.

But if choice is the forming of an intention based on deliberation about how to achieve what is best, we must be clear about the nature of deliberation. Intention, the genus to which choice belongs, was explained in Chapter I of Book III; choice is defined as being that intention which is based on deliberation in Chapter 2; being so based is its difference, that distinguishes it from other species of the genus, intention; deliberation will be explained in Chapter 3. Such is the plan of this section of the work.

DELIBERATION

Deliberation, Aristotle holds, must always be towards some envisaged goal that is possible of achievement. Thus, one does not deliberate about the universe or the incommensurability of the side and diagonal of a square. As Carlyle is alleged to have commented about the lady who said that she accepted the universe, 'Gad, she'd better'. What inevitably will happen will happen and there is no deliberating about it. Also one may have pipe dreams about things which are under the control of other people, but one cannot deliberate about such things; I cannot deliberate about where you will go for your next holidays. Again, there is no possibility of deliberation regarding matters that happen unpredictably, such as droughts and earthquakes or matters of chance – one cannot deliberate about whether to find a hoard of buried treasure (1112b 27). Deliberation has a rational place only in matters what are within our own control, and even here, Aristotle holds, deliberation is needed only when there is no well-known standard way of achieving one's purpose. Aristotle gives dated examples to illustrate this point (1112b 5);

to use a modern example, we might deliberate about how best to get from London to Liverpool by road, but not about how to start the car's engine.

Aristotle now makes an important and puzzling point. He says that we deliberate about how to achieve our ends, but do not deliberate about the ends themselves (1112b 11–12). This seems to be a surprising statement; one might protest that a young man or woman will very likely deliberate about ends at the beginning of his or her career. The question arises whether to aim to be a doctor, or lawyer, butcher or baker or candlestick-maker. This issue might well be thought to require at least as much careful deliberation as the problem how to achieve one's chosen end. This point is so obvious that it would be surprising if even a much lesser intelligence than Aristotle possessed were to miss it. We must try to understand Aristotle's doctrine more exactly before we accuse him of so simple an error.

Aristotle's own words are: 'We do not deliberate about ends, but about how to achieve them. For a doctor does not deliberate whether he will cure nor an orator whether he will convince, nor a statesman whether he will establish good government, nor does anyone else deliberate about his end. But having laid down an end they consider how and by what means it will be attained' (1112b 11–16).

Most commonly, Aristotle is interpreted as saying that by having become a doctor one has already adopted a policy of treating illnesses, and similarly in other cases. A doctor is not entitled, or expected, to ask whether to aid the sick, but he may well have to deliberate about how to set about doing it. The trouble with this interpretation is that Aristotle is now being taken to say that once one has chosen to be a physician there is no need to deliberate whether to practise one's profession. But then, we may retort, Aristotle is merely saying that once one point has been settled deliberation about it is no longer necessary. When one has, perhaps after long deliberation, chosen to become a physician, further deliberation about whether to treat patients is unnecessary, necessary only about how best to do it. If this is Aristotle's view he has expressed it very badly. Instead of saying what he has been quoted as saying above, he should have said something like: 'We deliberate first what ends to aim at and once that is settled we need to deliberate only about how to achieve them'. But this is very unlike what he in fact did say.

There is a better interpretation of Aristotle, which makes sense of his statement. It will be remembered that in the previous chapter Aristotle said that we choose a way to achieve our end but not the end itself, stating that it does not make sense to talk of choosing to be healthy or, in general, to succeed in anything. Success is what we aim at, wish for, not what we choose. I think that Aristotle is here making the same point about deliberation that he has already made about choice. One can choose to apply to go to medical school, perhaps after deliberating whether to apply, but one cannot choose that the application be accepted, a success not in one's control. One can deliberate about how to work for one's medical examinations, but not whether to succeed in passing them. Once one has become a physician, one no longer needs to deliberate about whether to treat patients, though one could; what one cannot do is to choose to be successful in curing them. Similarly, a political speaker may deliberate whether he should advocate some policy; but he cannot deliberate about whether he will be successful in attracting votes for it. In each case one can deliberate only about one's strategy and tactics. Very often, where translators speak of 'ends', it is better to substitute the word 'success'; if we follow that policy we shall not quote Aristotle as holding that one deliberates and chooses means but not ends, but rather as holding that we can deliberate about and choose a course of action that we hope, and perhaps expect, to be successful, but we cannot deliberate or choose whether to be successful. So interpreted, Aristotle's doctrine no longer sounds paradoxical, but sober common sense. Most of the examples that he gives of ends are such that involve success, such as health, victory, curing, convincing and, pre-eminently, eudaemonia.

Anything may be a success in a suitably framed situation. Thus, if one moves one's hand in order to pick up a spoon, Aristotle would certainly regard the motion of one's hand as a deliberately chosen means towards an end. Moving one's hand is something so plainly within one's power in normal circumstances that we can obviously choose to do so. But it is easy to imagine a person who has suffered some paralysing illness or accident who might struggle to move his hand and for whom to move it might be a surprising success which he could not simply choose to achieve.

As to whether we can choose to try to achieve some success or deliberate about whether to try to achieve it, Aristotle says nothing explicit; but he would surely agree that we can. Indeed, he insists over and over again that the aim of the *Nicomachean Ethics* is practical, not theoretical, and that it is to help us to determine what sort of life we should aim at, to decide what sort of success in life to aim at. Having decided what sort of life is the best, we can surely choose to try to achieve it, though not, of course, to succeed in doing so.

Aristotle has told us what matters lie within the scope of deliberation. He goes on to tell us in what deliberation consists. Having a goal or end in view, we first ask what final step will best and most easily enable us to achieve it (1112b 16-17); if that step is not immediately within our power, we ask by what prior step we may achieve it and so on until we come to something within our power. At that stage deliberation ends and action begins. He also notes that there may be more than one way of reaching the goal, in which case we have further to determine which route is preferable.

Aristotle draws an analogy between deliberation and analysis in geometry; he assumes that we know what this is, and does not elaborate. What he has in mind is something like this: let us suppose that the problem is how to construct a rectangle in a circle with the aid of a ruler and compasses; the final step to achieving this will be to determine four equidistant points on the circumference to be joined into a square; to do that one had best draw two diameters at right angles to each other, and to do that one must first draw some arbitrary diameter; that is directly in one's power, and action begins.

In the next chapter of Book III, the fourth, Aristotle has something to say about the relation of rational wish to choice and deliberation; these are not of the end or success, but wish is. Aristotle conceives of there being two ultimate types of goal, the good and the pleasant. Everything that we want will be either good or pleasant. The pleasant can be sought without any thought, deliberation or choice, which is why irrational animals are immediately stimulated into action by the appetite for the pleasant. But the good can be determined only by calculating effects over time and balancing advantages against disadvantages. So the psychology of action in outline is that one may desire the good, which is wish, or the pleasant, which is appetite; if the desire is for the pleasant and it is immediately attainable we may seek it, like any animal, without thought; if it is not within our immediate grasp we may have to deliberate how to attain it. If the desire is for the good, then there must have been thought to determine that it is good; if it is, it may be immediately attainable without thought, or it may require deliberation and choice of how to attain it.

THE GOOD AND THE APPARENT GOOD

But there is a problem about saying that rational wish is for the good, and Aristotle raises it in this chapter; it had already exercised Plato and various other philosophers and sophists. The problem is whether we do in fact wish for the good or, rather, for what seems to us to be good. There are very plausible arguments for and against each of these alternatives. Since it is always possible to make a mistake in trying to determine what is good, we should surely not agree that somebody wished for the good if we were sure that he had made a mistake and that in fact what he wished for was bad; we could also never be sure that anyone had a rational wish if wish is defined as for the good and error about the good is always possible. But if we choose the other alternative and say that wish is not for the good but only for the apparent good, there is an equally potent difficulty; if asked whether what we want, what we wish for, is just what seems to us to be good or what really is good, we should surely answer that it was the truly good. If, on a journey, one chooses what seems to be the best route, loses one's way, but luckily hits on a better one, one will be glad. One wanted to travel the best route and hit on it by chance.

Aristotle, characteristically and surely correctly, solves the problem by saying that each answer is, taken in an appropriate way, correct. But his explanation is, in detail, not entirely clear and satisfactory. In his usual tentative and undogmatic style he writes: 'Should we say that in an unqualified way and in truth the good is what is wished for, but by each individual what seems to be good?' (1113a 23–24). This is not entirely clear or convincing, and perhaps Aristotle had not available the kind of conceptual apparatus necessary to solve the problem in a clear manner. To do so requires the distinction between what in the philosophy of language are called the intentional and the extensional reading of statements of the form 'X wishes for Y'.

It is easy to construct analogues to this problem. Thus, let us suppose that I go out, as I honestly claim, on a tiger hunt. I come upon the spoor of a leopard, ignorantly mistake it for the spoor of a tiger and follow the spoor. The question is whether I am hunting a tiger or hunting a leopard. Once again, the same problem arises. Surely I know perfectly well that I have set out on a tiger hunt, not a leopard hunt; it is tiger not leopard that I want to bag; but you, the expert, know equally well that there are no tigers around and that I am in fact pursuing a leopard. There are many similar problems; thus I may claim to be looking for money in my purse when in fact the purse is empty, so that it might seem that I am looking for nothing.

A little reflection on the principles involved in cases like this should lead us to a solution of the problem. We must distinguish between a correct description of the agent's intention, his project, and a correct description of the facts. Always it will be true and a correct description of his intentions that he wishes for the good, is hunting tiger, is looking for money; only sometimes will it be true that there is something that is both good and the object of his wish, something that is a tiger and the object he is hunting, something that is money and the object of his search. In the jargon I have already mentioned, the good, the tiger, and money are the intentional object of the verb, but not always the extensional object.

So we can agree with Aristotle that both the thesis that we wish for the good and the thesis that wish for what seems good are each true taken correctly. The good is the intentional object of our wish, the apparent good is the extensional object. Probably Aristotle is searching for some such account as this, but what he says is too obscure to be interpeted with certainty.

FREEDOM

Chapter 5 of Book III of the *Nicomachean Ethics* stands on its own. The first four chapters have presupposed that in general we are responsible for our actions, that we intend them and can be properly praised or blamed for them. The first chapter discussed the exceptions to this presupposition, where intention was absent and praise and blame were inappropriate. The next three chapters, based on this presupposition, have discussed the various elements in the planning and choice of actions and the relation of such planning and choice to the envisaged goal or success. After Chapter 5 the whole topic of the psychology of action is dropped and Aristotle turns to an examination, one by one, of the various specific excellences of character.

But in this chapter Aristotle examines the presupposition of the previous chapters. In so doing he is facing the set of problems collectively called the problem of free will. Aristotle is often said to have been unaware of this problem, and it is true that he does not approach it against a background either of theological predestination or of scientific determinism, as is typically the case in later times. But to me it seems obvious that he is concerned with the same basic issues, and achieves the same degree of success, or lack of success, as anyone else.

Aristotle has already, in fact, touched on this basic problem of responsibility for action, but has not taken it very seriously. Thus, he mentions those who say that pleasant and even good things have forced them to act in the way they did (1110b 9-17), but replies curtly that this will make everything that one does a forced action, whereas what one does with pleasure is the paradigm case of intended and willing action. A page or two later he rejects the view that when appetite and spirit (anger) lead to action that action should be counted as unintended (1111a 23 ff) with roughly the same response.

But in Chapter 5 the problem is treated seriously. Aristotle starts by reiterating the common-sense result at which he has arrived. The successes that we wish for and what we plan to do and choose to do to achieve these successes are paradigm cases of intended action for which we are to be held responsible. He adds a point that is surely obvious when pointed out but often missed by people untrained in philosophy. If it is in our power to act, it is in our power to refrain from action and if it is in our power to act rightly, then it is in our power to act wrongly. People are liable to forget this point, though it is obvious; they excuse the thief, the vandal and the wastrel, saying they are the helpless products of their heredity and environment, but still continue to admire and praise the adherents of what they regard as good causes and to censure those who do not so excuse criminals. But they should either blame the thieves and the vandals, or say that adherents to good causes are mere helpless products of genetic and social factors. If consistency is genetically produced we should select for it.

But at 1114a Aristotle begins to face up to the difficulties. He himself has told us that we are born without a character and that we acquire a character through training. Thus, it can appear that others are responsible for our having the character we have, and thus it is they, rather than we ourselves, who are responsible for the actions we do in accordance with our character; we are, therefore without merit or fault.

Aristotle illustrates the point by considering what would normally be regarded as culpable ignorance. Ignorance itself may be culpable, even if that ignorance makes an act performed contrary to intention and therefore not itself blameworthy. We may accuse a man of culpable ignorance if, for example, he does not know that being drunk and disorderly is a crime. We may say that he ought to have known and would have known if he had taken a little trouble to ascertain the law. But why should he not say that he is not the sort of person to take that trouble – to do so would be out of character – he was not brought up to act that way? Aristotle's answer is that this may be so in some cases; we may become irremediably bad in many ways. But Aristotle holds that we may, nonetheless, be responsible for becoming that sort of person, just as one may become incurably ill but could have avoided, at an earlier stage, becoming so.

Aristotle attempts to justify this view by an appeal to reason. Even if I am brought up to be a wastrel who will, unless changed, end up in wretchedness and misery, it is possible for me, whatever training I have had, to recognize the facts and then retrain myself to better ways. One does not need to be abnormally clever to see this; heavy smokers, drug addicts and the overweight can well see where they are heading, can make an effort to reform and do sometimes succeed. Thus, Aristotle claims that we are partly responsible for our characters (1114b 22).

It may well be doubted whether this is a satisfactory final solution to the problem of responsibility if it is rigorously insisted on. One drug addict sees plainly where his addiction is leading him and makes the effort to reform; another sees equally plainly but does not make the effort. It is not clear how Aristotle, or anybody else, is to explain facts such as this. At the common-sense level it is obviously true that people can and do reform themselves and reshape their characters for better or worse and can thus be said to be partly responsible for their characters, but this fact does not remove the basic philosophical difficulties.

If we turn to the very last chapter of the final book of the *Nicomachean Ethics* we shall find Aristotle acknowledging that in the end we are lucky if we have the initial natural endowment to be easily trained into a good character (1179b 21) and if we are born into an environment that provides the right sort of training (1179b 23). But Aristotle would surely never have abandoned his claim in Book III that neither praise or blame can be deserved unless we are responsible for our actions. Some modern philosophers have claimed that praise and blame would serve as useful carrots and sticks to influence even nonresponsible men or donkeys; but that is a different matter.

5

Particular Excellences of Character

From Chapter 6 of Book III of the *Nichomachean Ethics* to the end of Book V Aristotle discusses the particular excellences of character, one by one. He has a dual aim. Most obviously, Aristotle thinks that it is part of the function of ethics to give an account of these excellences for their own sake; in doing so he started a practice of giving sketches of types of character which was to be much imitated, most immediately by his younger colleague, Theophrastus, in his still extant *Characters*. But also he endeavours continually to show that the excellences conform to his definition in Book II. He tries to show that each excellence is a mean state between two bad states with regard to feeling, and that each exhibits some specific emotion.

Aristotle rather optimistically says that this survey will also determine how many particular excellences of character there are. But, to determine this, one would have to have a clearer way of individuating emotions than Aristotle had, or we have nowadays, and some way of showing that the list had been exhausted.

To read through this catalogue of excellences is instructive; it reveals what must be a view of the ideal gentleman as visualized by Aristotle and, presumably, by many other upper- and middle-class Greeks of the fourth century BC. Some of the time we can easily sympathize; at other times we are inclined to be repelled. But most of the time there are few philosophical difficulties and it would be tedious for me to discuss them all, one by one. I shall, instead, concentrate on three of the most important excellences with regard to which puzzles do arise. These are bravery, temperance and justice.

BRAVERY

The first particular excellence discussed by Aristotle, and the first to be discussed here, is bravery. Bravery was a very important quality in the ancient city-state, which was liable to be constantly at war with its neighbours and where every man was a soldier who might well see active service. So important was bravery that a man was often called good or bad simply with reference to his prowess in battle.

It would have been easy for Aristotle to give a short, simple account of bravery that would have readily fitted in with the doctrine of the mean, rather than the long, complex, and often puzzling account that he does give. Let us supply in half a dozen lines this simple story that Aristotle does not give. Bravery, we say is concerned with the emotion of fear which one may feel and display too much or too little, and is the mean state between these extremes. The too fearful man is a coward, the too little fearful has no standard name, but might be called foolhardy; he is noted by Macbeth when he says:

I dare do all that may become a man;
Who dares do more is none.

Some of the puzzlement that readers experience when they read Aristotle's text is to be explained by the inadequacy of translation. 'Bravery', and still more 'courage', both of which are commonly used in translations, are wider and more inclusive terms than the Greek term that they attempt to render. Thus, Aristotle says that standard cases of bravery are displayed only in warfare and in the face of death (1115a 33–35); to apply the concept elsewhere is to extend it. So Aristotle's concept is narrower than ours; perhaps the rather archaic term 'valour' has this same restricted sense and would therefore be preferable to bravery or courage as a translation. Certainly no Greek would have included such things as a woman's courage in adversity, moral courage and the like under the concept; Aristotle's restriction is not arbitrary and reflects the usual Greek usage. However, for the rest of this discussion the terms 'bravery' and 'brave' will be retained in use, and the reader must be careful to understand them aright.

But Aristotle's treatment of the topic is puzzling in other ways also. Already in Book II he has said: 'Bravery is a mean with regard to fears and confidence. He who is excessively fearless has no name (there are many nameless states); he who exceeds in confidence is rash, he who is excessively fearful and too little confident is a coward' (1107a 33-b4). From this it appears that he who fears too little and is nameless is different from him who exceeds in confidence and is rash; the rash man is not nameless and must be different. But it appears that the coward is the opposite of both of these.

Now Aristotle's regular doctrine is that if a term has two different opposites it must be ambiguous; this is clearly stated in the *Topics* (106a 9–22), with two illustrations, and found frequently elsewhere. So, since the coward has two opposites, one the rash man, the other nameless, the term 'coward' ought to be ambiguous. Further, if the brave man is in a mean in each case, then 'brave' ought to be ambiguous also. If this be granted, then we get two triads like this:

Emotion	Excess	Mean	Deficiency
Fear	Coward	Brave	Nameless
Confidence	Rash	Brave	Coward

Thus the ambiguously named coward is either in an excess of fear or a deficiency of confidence. But Aristotle gives no indication that he recognizes any such ambiguity here. Perhaps it would have been better to recognize two triads of excellence and faults, two types of good and bad character thus:

Emotion	Excess	Mean	Deficiency
Fear	Coward	Brave	Nameless
Confidence	Rash	Cautious	Overcautious

But Aristotle does not, though it has much to commend it in its own right.

Aristotle's puzzling juxtaposition of fear and confidence can perhaps be explained by what he says at the beginning of Book III Chapter 6. There he states that bravery is a mean between fear and confidence; we fear what is fearful, which is what is bad. So fear is defined as the expectation of what is bad. We fear all bad things, but bravery is not concerned with them all.

Now let us consider the statement: 'I am afraid that England will lose the Test Match'. given that I am a partisan of England, that is a clear case of fear defined, as Aristotle says, as expectation of the bad. But this sort of fear has absolutely nothing to do with the sort of fear one might feel when in battle, riding a bicycle in Oxford, or in any other danger. If another supporter of England has no fear that England will lose, that does not make him brave, but it makes him confident. Again, if somebody is not afraid of the dark, this does not mean that he feels confident in the dark; normally he will not have any special feelings about the dark whatsoever. The sort of person who is likely to be comparatively confident in the dark is the congenitally blind man who has the skill, while the sighted man will be cautious, or even over-cautious, but not cowardly.

Confidence, then, seems to have nothing essential to do with the sort of fear or terror with which bravery and cowardice are concerned, though it is easy to see how confidence may in some situations result in the absence of terror. But a very brave man may be temperamentally overcautious and inclined to expect the worst. Perhaps Aristotle begins to recognize this point when he says at the end of his discussion of bravery that though it 'is concerned with confidence and fear, it is not concerned with both alike, but more with the things that inspire fear' (1117a 29–30).

So I think that Aristotle has made two errors. First, he has failed to distinguish the notion of fear as simply the expectation of evil and thus opposed to confidence, from the notion of fear as concerned with danger and having no essential connection with confidence. In the second place, he has failed to distinguish the triad concerned with fear of the dangerous – cowardice, bravery and the state he says is nameless, but might be called foolhardiness – from another triad the members of which might be called overconfidence, caution and overcautiousness.

There is another distinction with regard to fear and bravery that is very important and of which Aristotle does at least have some grasp. There is a great difference between on the one hand being afraid when one is in battle or riding a bicycle in Oxford and on the other being afraid to do battle or afraid to ride a bicycle in Oxford. Any sane man is going to be afraid from time to time in battle, but that does not make him a coward; cowardice is being afraid to do in battle that which is needful. The brave man will not be afraid to stand his ground, but will not be inclined to expose himself needlessly. This distinction is at least strongly suggested in such a passage as: 'Now the brave man is as dauntless as man may be. Therefore, while he will fear even the things that are not beyond human strength, he will face them as he ought and as is reasonable for honour's sake' (1115b 10–13). The suggestion often attributed to Aristotle that brave men are liable to experience fear only in the face of dangers that it would be unreasonable to expect them to face is really bizarre and shows a remarkable ignorance of human nature of which Aristotle is not guilty.

There is one final difficulty that Aristotle has to face. He has said in his general account of excellence of character that the man of excellent character likes, enjoys, takes pleasure in performing excellent actions. But bravery, he recognizes, may involve facing distress, wounds and the prospect of death. So, he concludes that, contrary to the general rule, not all excellent activity is pleasant (1117b 15–16). But he tries to rescue at least a modified version of the doctrine. The brave man may find the action entailed distressing, but, like the boxer who willingly accepts painful blows, he acts as he does because the goal is pleasant. He positively wants to act honourably and dreads the thought of acting shamefully.

I think that Aristotle does succeed in saving what is most important in his general account of excellence of character. Though he has had to withdraw the claim that the action will always be positively pleasant, it remains that there will be no internal friction as there will be in the strong-willed man, who has to make himself act properly. The brave man does not want to run away and does not have to force himself to stand his ground. In this way he is like the boxer, the long-distance runner, the mountaineer and many others who want to do what they do in spite of the danger, fatigue and pain that they have to endure. That the man of excellent character wants to act as he does is surely a more important element in the Aristotelian doctrine than that he finds the action positively enjoyable.

TEMPERANCE

Temperance is discussed by Aristotle immediately after bravery in the final two chapters of Book III of the *Nicomachean Ethics*. It is concerned with a restricted range of pleasures, of which pre-eminent examples are those of eating, drinking and sex. It is a mean between self-indulgence on the one hand and an insensitivity to such pleasures which he considers to be very rare and therefore discusses very little. It is certainly rare, it is absurd to call it a vice, but Aristotle is surely right in thinking that there is something wrong with the person who does not enjoy even the sober meals that are required to maintain health and strength. The word 'temperance' as used in modern English has a more restricted sense than is needed here and as used here should be regarded as a dummy translation doing duty in the lack of a better.

The main interest in Aristotle's discussion of temperance is to see Aristotle struggling to make important theoretical distinctions within the concept of pleasure which the pre-philosophical Greek language was ill-equipped to make and which modern philosophers still often fail to observe.

If we say that all excellences of character are concerned with pleasure in so far as (neglecting Aristotle's difficulties with bravery) all excellent activities are pleasant, temperance is concerned with pleasure doubly. For while other excellences are concerned with the proper feeling and exhibition of fear, anger, pity, etcetera, temperance is concerned with the proper feeling and exhibition of a desire for certain pleasures, such as those of eating, drinking and sex.

Aristotle's first task is to isolate and define those pleasures with which temperance is concerned. To that end he starts by

distinguishing mental and bodily pleasures (1117b 28–29).
Mental pleasures include such pleasures as those of the pursuit of
knowledge and the pursuit of honour, which, Aristotle says, do
not involve the body in any way. Bodily pleasures, as Aristotle
defines them, constitute a wider class then we usually think of as
being bodily, since he includes all that involve the use of the
senses. Thus, all pleasures that involve the use of sight and
hearing are classed as bodily, whereas we should not normally
think of the visitor to an art gallery as being in pursuit of bodily
pleasure. But Aristotle recognizes that such pleasures as these are
irrelevant to the excellence of temperance. Thus, listening to
music is classed by him as a bodily pleasure since it is an exercise
of the sense of hearing. But while listening to music may be bad,
if carried to excess, this is not thought of in the same way as
excessive eating and drinking. Aristotle concludes that the true
sphere of temperance is the pleasures of touch. In so far as
temperance is concerned with other senses, it is because they are
associated with the pleasures of touch, as the smell of food is
associated with eating it. This conclusion is not offered as an
arbitrary fiat. Aristotle claims that the terms 'temperate' and
'self-indulgent' are applied only with reference to the pleasures of
touch, and that he is noting an accepted distinction and making
explicit the rule for the use of words that people already follow.
Though our English words are only roughly equivalent to the
Greek, we perhaps think in much the same way as Aristotle
indicates.

We might well wonder why the pleasures of touch should have
a special excellence of character connected with them, whereas it
appears that the pleasures of the other senses do not. Why, for
example, is there not a special excellence of character connected
with the pleasures of using the sense of sight, or of hearing? That
is what we must try to answer.

I think that the class of pleasures that Aristotle is endeavour-
ing to pick out as the field of temperance is that of bodily
sensations. There is a crude view, not yet dead, that to call
anything pleasant is to say that it produces some special feeling
called a feeling of pleasure. Aristotle shows no sign of believing
any such absurdity. In his view the pleasure of learning, for

example, is a pleasure, not because it produces a pleasant feeling of any sort, let alone a feeling itself called pleasure, but because the acquisition of knowledge is intrinsically pleasant. Such a pleasure is classed as non-bodily because it is not essentially linked with the exercise of any sense, though if in fact we had no senses we, no doubt, could acquire no knowledge. Such pleasures as those of listening to music or looking at pictures are classed as bodily because they do essentially require the use of a sense. One could not listen to music without the sense of hearing or look at pictures without the sense of sight. Aristotle believes that touch, such as the stimulation of the organs of sex can produce bodily feelings which are pleasant in themselves, just as listening to music is pleasant in itself. In neither case do we need to posit a special feeling of pleasure. The field of temperance is then these pleasant feeling induced in our bodies by touch.

That this is Aristotle's view is confirmed by his ambivalence about the sense of taste. He does in fact say that the sphere of temperance is touch and taste. He is inclined to think of taste as a type of touch, since it involves contact, unlike hearing, sight and even smell; in *On the Soul (De anima)* he refers to a flavour as something touched (414b 6–11). But taste is only regarded as relevant when it is used for acquiring pleasant sensations; the critical use of taste, as in judging wine or cookery, is something quite different, and irrelevant to temperance.

A lot more will have to be said about Aristotle's general doctrine of pleasure when we come to consider his full discussions of it in Books VII and X. In particular we need to know what account he will give of those sorts of pleasure that are not pleasant bodily feelings. The commentator, Aspasius, writing in the early second century AD, was particularly puzzled by Aristotle's claim at 1179b 30–31 that there were mental pleasures involving nothing bodily or emotional. 'What does he mean', he wrote, 'when he says that lovers of learning and honour enjoy them by their intelligence being affected? For enjoyment and pleasures are not in the intelligence but in the emotional element in the soul'. This is a question that should be asked and one that Aristotle will answer, but not while he is discussing temperance.

It may be thought that Aristotle's way of making the distinction he requires, by connecting temperance with the sense of touch is not theoretically sound, even if it points us in the right direction. For it seems clear that there can be pleasures involving the sense of touch that have as little to do with temperance as do those of sight and hearing; examples might be the pleasure of feeling the wind on one's face on a hot, muggy day or the pleasure of feeling the texture and shape of surfaces, which can be so important to the blind and are not unknown to others.

What we need is a distinction between the enjoyment of a bodily state produced by contact with an object and the enjoyment of feeling an object. The blind man feeling a statue with his hands is not trying to induce pleasant bodily sensations. Moreover, it is only an empirical question whether hearing certain sounds might not induce in us feelings of a sort that are in the field of temperance and self-indulgence. The basic distinction is between the enjoyment of the exercise of a sense, whether it be touch, sight, or any other, and enjoyment of feelings produced by the exercise of a sense.

Aristotle obviously feels a special contempt for self-indulgence. The self-indulgent man is not even excessive with regard to distinctively human activities, but in the satisfaction of appetites that we share with beasts (1118b 1–4). But Aristotle is not an ascetic; his temperate man will enjoy his food and other bodily pleasures so far as they are needful, fitting, and within his means (1119a 16–18). Such pleasures are natural, and Aristotle never regards what is natural as in principle bad. He nowhere condemns our natural emotions and desires, and he knows that we are animals, even if we are rational ones. With temperance, as with all other excellencies of character, what is wrong is excess and deficiency; there is nothing wrong with the appetites themselves.

JUSTICE

Aristotle's discussion of justice is much more elaborate than that of any other excellence of character, occupying the whole of Book V of the *Nicomachean Ethics*. It contains a number of penetrating discussions that have had so much influence that they may now seem sometimes to state the obvious. Aristotle's works are full of platitudes in much the same way as Shakespeare's *Hamlet* is full of quotations. But it is hard to see it as a successfully organized whole, and in so far as it aims to depict justice as an excellence of character exemplifying the doctrine of the mean – as a mean state with regard to feeling and exhibiting some specific emotion – it fails on his own admission (1133b 33–34). But it is, nonetheless, fruitful reading.

Aristotle begins by correctly pointing out that the Greek words we translate by 'justice' and 'injustice' are ambiguous. Since these English words are not ambiguous, or, at least, not in the way the Greek words are, this claim is not immediately convincing in translation. The unjust man, he says, may be, on the one hand, a man who is in general lawless, or he may be, specifically, the man who is unfair and grasping, who aims to get more than his fair share.

These two meanings and the confusion the ambiguity can cause, may be illustrated from the first book of Plato's *Republic*. There Polemarchus offers the definition that justice is rendering to each man what is due to him; this is surely at least a reasonable shot at defining justice in Aristotle's narrower sense. But Socrates offers as a counterexample to this definition that it is unjust to return a borrowed weapon to a man who has gone mad. Now it may be imprudent, reckless, negligent and even unkind to return the weapon in the envisaged circumstances; but it would not in English naturally be called unjust to return it, nor would it be unfair or grasping to do so. Polemarchus' correct reply would be that it is not unjust in the narrower sense to return the weapon, but he gives way just because the ambiguity was present in ancient Greek, undetected by him. Socrates was a past master at trading on ambiguities, and Aristotle at exposing them.

Justice in the wider sense, for which a better term in English might be 'righteousness', is, Aristotle says, the same thing as excellence of character and injustice the same thing as badness of character, but the expressions are not synonymous. In so far as we are interested in the nature of the agent, we speak in terms of excellence or badness of character; in so far as we are interested in the way his actions affect other people, we speak in terms of justice and injustice (1130a 8–13). In Book V Aristotle will not usually be concerned with justice in the wider sense, called by him 'complete justice', but with what he calls 'particular justice', which is specifically concerned with people getting their fair shares.

The discussion of particular justice begins in earnest at 1130b 30. So far, we have been told that the characteristic of the unjust man is to aim at more than his fair share, but now we might expect the same sort of general account that is given for the other particular excellences. We might, as in the case of other excellences, expect to be told what the particular emotion involved is and what the two extremes are between which justice is an excess, one exhibiting too much, the other too little, of the relevant emotion. But this we do not get, and never will get; and it is quite obvious why. If injustice is aiming at more than one's fair share and justice, presumably, aiming at one's fair share, we cannot get such an account. For whatever is wrong – if anything – with aiming at less than one's fair share, it cannot be called unjust, particularly by Aristotle who, as we shall find (1138a 15), denies that one can be unjust to oneself.

What we get instead is a discussion of what is called particular justice, but it is very different from what would satisfy such expectations. Instead we find justice subdivided into two types, called distributive and rectificatory justice. Very briefly stated, distributive justice is concerned with ensuring a proper distribution of honour and wealth among the citizens, rectificatory justice is concerned with restoring fair shares when some unfairness has come about.

Within rectificatory justice Aristotle then makes further subdivisions of some importance. The need for rectificatory justice may arise with regard to transactions that are intended or those that are contary to intention. In traditional translations these appear as 'voluntary' and 'involuntary transactions'. As examples of intended transactions he lists buying and selling, loans, deposits, leasing and the like – agreements that two or more parties have chosen to make. Within transactions contrary to intention he makes a further distinction between those arising through stealth and those arising through force. Examples of those involving stealth are burglary, adultery, false witness and poisoning; examples of those involving force are assault, wounding, murder and kidnaping.

Before we go further, we might usefully remind ourselves of some features of modern law. Here, in addition to certain irrelevant types, such as constitutional law, we have a fundamental distinction between civil and criminal law. In civil law one person may claim damages from another person; there is no prosecutor and no accused but an appellant and a defendant; there is no conviction or punishment, but damages may be awarded to a successful appellant. Moreover, the individual who has been wronged brings the case to the courts himself at his own discretion; there is no Director of Public Prosecutions or District Attorney involved, nor any similar functionary. If the defendant loses, he is not thereby a criminal. Within civil law there is a further distinction of contract and tort; the area of contract is very similar to that which is occupied by Aristotle's intended transactions. The area of tort includes at least some of the examples that Aristotle gives of transactions contrary to intention, since civil cases can be brought for such things as slander, assault and even theft, though some examples in Aristotle's list, such as murder, fall exclusively under criminal law, while others can become the subject of criminal prosecution as well as of civil suit.

In contrast to civil law, criminal law provides for the prosecution, usually by agents of the state, of persons accused of crimes for which, if found guilty, they are liable to punishment. The criminal may be ordered to make some restitution in cases such as theft, but essentially there is punishment, not restitution. Murderers do not pay restitution, and fines go to the state, not the party harmed.

It is clear that neither Aristotle's distributive justice nor his rectificatory justice falls neatly into our modern categories of civil and criminal justice. But it is of some interest to look for both similarities and differences. It is immediately obvious, as their names suggest, that Aristotle's two types are both closer to civil than to criminal justice. Distributive justice, rather like a case in civil law concerning the distribution among claimants of the goods of a deceased person, aims at fair distribution among possible recipients and punishment is obviously totally irrelevant. Rectificatory justice, in restoring a distribution of goods to fairness, also sounds rather like the award of damages in a civil suit. It even seems that Aristotle's distinction of wrongs arising from intended and unintended transactions corresponds to our distinction of breach of contract and tort. This is not to suggest that the ancient Greeks had nothing similar to our criminal law, for they had. Socrates' condemnation to death for impiety and corrupting the young, for example, bears little resemblance to a civil, and much to a criminal, process as we know them today. But it also bears little resemblance to Aristotle's distributive and rectificatory justice. It would be as silly to deny the close resemblance of these to our law of contract and tort as it would be to try to claim that they were identical.

Aristotle's treatment of distributive justice is in its detail a reflection of the political institutions of his time and place. He treats it as being primarily concerned with the distribution of honours and wealth to citizens of the state. As has often been remarked this is to treat the citizen as a shareholder rather than a taxpayer. Making perhaps excessive use of elementary mathematics, Aristotle points out that a fair distribution will make the wealth or honour given proportional to the desert of the claimants. Desert will be determined by the political system in force, and in his ethical works, unlike those on politics, he does not adjudicate between them. If, as in an ancient democracy, all citizens are to be treated as equals, they will receive equal shares, if, as in an aristocracy, some are treated as more deserving, they will receive proportionately more. While a modern might think that, financially, extra desert would be judged in terms of need, there is no suggestion of such a procedure here. No doubt in modern Britain the distribution of honours still proceeds on such aristocratic or plutocratic principles as Aristotle envisages in financial matters.

But the Aristotelian notion of distributive justice is in principle important and can be easily modernized and extended in its scope. Modernized, it will be concerned with the distribution of tax burdens by the state. To determine the proper distribution of tax burdens we need some theory of desert; ought we, for example, to tax all men equally, as we do with most indirect taxes, or ought we to regard the rich (or the poor) as deserving to pay more (or less) tax? The notion of distributive justice can also be extended in scope, even to such trivial matters as, literally, dividing up the cake on the family table; should the holder of the knife give equal shares to all, or more to the biggest appetites or the best behaved, or act on yet some other principle of desert? It is clear that these questions raise important matters of principle. It is clear also that only distributors, whether of tax claims, cakes, or anything else, can exhibit the excellence of being just, or be unjust, in the field of distributive justice; the rest of us can in these matters only be treated justly or unjustly.

With regard to rectificatory justice, Aristotle has a more simple mathematical formula. If a person A has gained an unfair advantage over B, he who administers rectificatory justice must restore the just situation. Thus, in a very simple case, if A has borrowed £10 from B, rectificatory justice demands that it be returned and a rectifying judge will so order. But this is, of course, a very simple case, and Aristotle realizes that to award damages for a matter such as the loss of a limb is less easy; he himself says that to use the terms gain and loss in such cases is artificial (1132a 10–14). The problem is well known today and is still the same as when Aristotle wrote.

Aristotle's attempts to bring distributive and rectificatory justice within the scope of the doctrine of the mean are at times sophistical and, even so, are in the end, as he admits, unsuccessful. An example of the sophistical can be found at 1131b 16–20. Here, with regard to distribution, Aristotle says that the just distribution is a mean between one party getting too much and another too little; he then actually says that the recipient of an unfairly large share is acting unjustly whereas he is obviously entirely passive and not an agent. In Book III he would be classed as acting at least unintentionally. Aristotle's confession of failure is to be found at 1133b 30–1134a 15. It is an important passage needing careful reading and runs as follows:

> "It is clear that just action is a mean between acting unjustly and suffering injustice; for the one is to have too much, the other to have too little. So justice is a mean, but not in the same way as other excellences, but because it aims at the mean and injustice at the extremes. And justice is that by which the just man is said to do by choice what is just and to be one who will distribute either between himself and another or between two others . . . so as to give what is proportionately fair".

Acting unjustly has already been denatured by being treated as merely having an unfair share; similarly just action is also denatured by being treated as merely having a fair share. Moreover, the just man is he who makes a fair distribution and the unjust he who makes an unfair distribution. So if A distributes unfairly by giving too much to B and too little to C, then A is unjust, B acts unjustly and C is unjustly treated. But if A were unjust one would think that he acted unjustly; but on this occasion he got nothing, while acting unjustly has been said to be getting an unfair share.

So Aristotle has got himself into a sophistical muddle, but has still not saved the day, since he admits that justice is not like the other excellences; it is said to aim at a mean, but this is true only if acting unjustly is implausibly reduced to getting more than one's fair share. He does, indeed, somewhat decrease the absurdity of his position by saying that it is possible to act unjustly without being unjust (1134a 17ff). But now acting unjustly is no longer implausibly treated as merely receiving too much but as positively acting in a way that gives one an unfair advantage, and being unjust is no longer to make an unfair distribution but to act unjustly with that intention and not merely incidentally in the prosecution of some different end.

It is not difficult to see what has gone wrong. Distributive and rectificatory justice, both of which can be manifested only by someone who is acting in a judicial or quasi-judicial capacity, simply are not excellences of character at all, nor are they manifestations of a single excellence of character. There is no special emotion that a judge ought to feel and exhibit to a right degree. Rather, he has to operate the principles of justice correctly, and to this end he has to be impartial, without fear or favour, even-tempered and, of course, clear-headed; in a word, he needs to be a man of generally good character, and not to display some special trait of character. The same is true of the schoolmaster, the government official and all in responsible positions. Administering justice is a special occupation, not a special character trait.

So Aristotle's failure to exhibit justice as an excellence of character is not very important. His account of distributive justice and rectificatory justice are not damaged by this failure, nor is his general account of excellence of character, once we see that Aristotle was making an unnecessary mistake in trying to link them together. Moreover, when he ceases to try to connect justice and the doctrine of the mean, he abandons his earlier sophisms. Thus, at 1136b 28 he says that it is clear that when injustice occurs it is the distributor who acts unjustly and not the person who has too much on each occasion, which is plainly right and flatly contradicts the passage at 1131b 16–20.

It was said above that no specific emotion was involved in either distributive or rectificatory justice. But at 1129a 32 Aristotle has suggested that particular injustice involves aiming at too great a share, as though it were the relevant emotion. But, in the first place, the distributor, or rectifier, who alone is capable of displaying these types of justice, may not get any share at all. Aristotle tries to get round this by saying that the unjust judge may aim at an unfair share of favour or revenge (1137a 1), but this is surely mere verbal juggling. We might as well treat the coward as unjust since he aims at an unfair share of safety; we might in this way be able to reduce all defects of character to greed.

If Aristotle wishes to make greed an example of a defect of character he will have to dissociate it from his particular justice. He will have to take some neutral emotion, perhaps called possessiveness or acquisitiveness, of which greed would be the excess. But now the problem will be how to find a plausible defect or deficiency, for being willing to forgo that to which you have a right is thought by Aristotle to be a sign of liberality or even magnificence. The best we can do is perhaps to suggest that the fault is not to be willing to forgo what one has a right to, but rather to have too low a view of one's rights. Such a man will resemble the unduly humble man as described at 1125a 17ff, who has in general too low an opinion of his own worth. But perhaps it would be pointless to multiply particular excellences by having a different one with regard to claims in different fields – claims to honour, claims to wealth and so on.

It is clear that to claim too small a share, even if a fault, is not injustice. This follows from an excellent point made by Aristotle that has become a recognized principle of law. He makes a distinction between harming somebody and treating him unjustly (1136b 5–6); in the legal tag, it is the distinction between *damnum* and *injuria*. For there to be *injuria* the *damnum*, or loss, must not be consented to. So taking to oneself the *damnum* consisting in too small a share cannot be a form of injustice. One cannot be unjust to oneself, just as one cannot steal from oneself or break a contract with oneself, whatever idiomatic talk there may be about doing oneself justice and the like.

There are other interesting discussions in Book V that will not be discussed here in depth. There is the discussion of the principle of reciprocity at 1132b 21 ff. Here Aristotle denies that, any more than the doctrine of an eye for an eye, it can be taken as straightforward principle of justice. But it has its place as the principle governing exchange of goods and in particular the use of money as a means facilitating exchange. As such, the discussion is no doubt elementary, but, when considered as a pioneering essay on economic theory, it can be seen to have merits. Another influential discussion is of the need for equity as a means of deciding issues unprovided for, or badly provided for, by law (1137a 31ff). These passages are left undiscussed here, not because they are negligible but because they are easily intelligible passages to which I have nothing useful to add. The treatment of justice must, considered as a whole, be judged a failure, both in its main contention and through its lack of a coherent organization. But, as should be abundantly clear, there are many discussions of particular topics that are both interesting in themselves and very influential on the development of law in western countries.

6

The Excellences of Intelligence

In this chapter we are concerned with what are traditionally known as the intellectual virtues, but will here be called excellences of intelligence. To count such an attribute as being good at geometry, which is certainly one of the sorts of thing that Aristotle had in mind, an excellence is reasonable; to call it a virtue is, in modern English, at best misleading. If today we speak of intellectual virtues they will naturally be such things as candour, impartiality and self-criticism, which are not the sorts of thing that Aristotle is about to discuss.

Book VI of the *Nicomachean Ethics*, in which excellences of intelligence are discussed, seems to get off to a false start. In the first section of the first chapter Aristotle clearly states that he is about to examine the nature of the principles of right reason that determine the mean between excess and deficiency (1138b 18–34). The remainder of the chapter, however, ignores this section; it states that there are two types of excellence of intelligence and proposes an examination of them which is begun in Chapter 3 and continues for the rest of the book. Nowhere does Aristotle tackle the problem set out in the first section of Chapter 1 and we shall later have to ask why. Meanwhile that section should be regarded as probably either a false start by Aristotle or an unfortunate editorial insertion.

The field of reason, Aristotle says, is truth. Pure theoretical reason is concerned with truth for its own sake. Aristotle conceives of it as a deductive system. We grasp certain basic truths immediately, such as the principle that a proposition and its contradictory cannot both be true; from them we deduce further truths. This is the procedure from first principles that Aristotle regards as providing true knowledge. Other sorts of theoretical reasoning, such as that to first principles, which he has said must be his method in the *Ethics* (1095b 3–4), are regarded as no more than provisional or preliminary.

There is a manifest gap in this account of theoretical reasoning, roughly corresponding to what we would call the empirical sciences. Theoretical reason is said to be concerned with what cannot be otherwise, what is as it is from necessity, what is eternally so (1139b 20–23). What can be otherwise is said to be within the spheres of action and production (1140a 1). Aristotle certainly did hold some basic scientific truths to be necessarily so and some processes, such as the movement of the heavens, to be everlastingly unchanging; but if we consider, for example, the many biological truths known to Aristotle, it is unclear how he would classify them. Moreover, if we look at Aristotle's own theoretical works, such as the *Metaphysics* and the *Physics*, they by no means conform to the deductive paradigm.

But reason in the practical sphere, while aiming at truth, is in the service of action. Chapter 2 of Book VI rehearses what we already know from earlier books. We already know that desire, whether it be wish or appetite, is for some end and that to achieve this end we have to choose some course of action that is immediately within our power. It is within the province of practical reason to determine, in the light of sound practical principles and a knowledge of the situation, what action to choose. So reason and desire are inseparable aspects of choice. There can be no choice without both a desire for an end and a reasoning about how to achieve it.

Excellence in theoretical matters is traditionally called wisdom in translations and excellence in practical matters is called practical wisdom. We shall adhere to that custom, though in contexts not connected with translation from Greek the terms 'wisdom' and 'wise' always have a practical connotation on their own. If we do refer to a wise mathematician, for example, it will be with reference to his practical approach to his work and not to his mathematical ability; also we speak of wise advice, plans and actions, not of wise theorems or theories.

Aristotle's treatment of practical wisdom does not consist, as the very opening of Book VI would suggest, of a catalogue of truths known to the practically wise man. Rather it consists of a series of descriptions of the various subordinate excellences of intelligence subsumed in practical wisdom.

First of all, a mark of practical wisdom is a capacity to plan one's life well (1140a 24–28). Deliberation has already been discussed in Chapter 3 of Book III and Aristotle repeats some of the points made there; one cannot make plans about what is necessarily so or is out of one's control. To be wise is an excellence; it is the disposition to judge rightly about human goods (1140b 21–22). Since practical wisdom is an excellence of this sort it cannot be possessed by a bad man. A bad man can work out well enough how to achieve his ends and so be a good planner, but his planning is not towards a good end and hence he will have suffered a great evil (1142b 18–20). But a wise man does not plan evil for himself. It may sound arbitrary to limit this excellence of intelligence to the good man, but we speak the same way in modern English. A crooked lawyer may be as clever as you please, but we cannot call him a wise lawyer. Again, no plan would be called wise, however ingenious, if it led to disaster. So wise planning and deliberation have to satisfy two criteria; they must conduce to the desired end and the end must be good, that is, it must lead towards eudaemonia. This, of course, implies that one cannot have practical wisdom unless one also has an excellent character. Aristotle will argue this more fully later, and we shall postpone our discussion of it until we have a fuller account of practical wisdom before us.

It is a superficial, but surprisingly common, mistake to suppose that the scope of practical wisdom is limited to excellence in deliberation; this is by no means so, for much more is involved. Chapters 10 and 11 of Book VI introduce us to two further subordinate excellences that, like deliberative ability, are requisite for practical wisdom. First there is understanding, the capacity to sum up a situation. But this, on its own, may be merely a touchline skill, whereas practical wisdom is, so to speak, exhibited on the field of play; it involves appreciating one's situation and knowing how to act accordingly while engaged in action (1143a 8–10). There is also judgement, the ability to determine, having sized up a situation, what is right and proper. Sound general principles on their own, are not enough; we need to be able to judge rightly all the complexities of concrete situations. This is something that comes only with experience (1143b 11–14). Incidentally, Aristotle holds that, in general, practical wisdom comes only with experience and riper years; but theoretical excellence, he notes, can be displayed by the very young. This is surely true; we all know of many cases of youthful prodigies in chess, in mathematics and in similar pursuits; but perhaps nobody would choose a teenager to represent him in a serious case in the law courts.

The last sentence of Chapter 11 suggests that the account of practical wisdom is now complete. But this is not so; for there is a further capacity which Aristotle explicitly says (1144a 28–29) is requisite for practical wisdom. This is cleverness, as we traditionally translate it, but we should look carefully at how Aristotle defines it. It is, he says, 'such that a person can accomplish those things that tend towards the proposed goal and achieve that goal' (1144a 24–26). That is what Aristotle says; its meaning is clear and is manifestly not the same as 'such that a person plans and deliberates well towards the proposed goal'. Cleverness is thus clearly not the same thing as deliberative and planning skill, but has its place after deliberation has terminated and the plan has been made. As Aristotle defines it, it is an executive and not a planning ability. Executive ability is not the exclusive prerogative of the wise man; a rogue may have it (1144a 27), but it is requisite for practical wisdom.

We must not underestimate the difference between planning and execution. In war, an officer may be a fine member of the planning staff, invaluable in producing plans for an operation; but a commanding general has to put these plans into operation, and not every skilled planner is able to do this. Again, it is one thing for a government to plan good laws; it is another thing to get them through a legislature. Part of knowing how to get things done is, no doubt, mainly a matter of having the requisite information, like, for example, the knowledge how to operate a word processor; but in varying degrees in various situations knowing how to recognize the right time to act, the right approach, the right place and so on, can be of vital importance, and even the best informed person may lack this knowledge. Making a plan and successfully putting it into operation are two very different things, both of which, Aristotle holds, are requisite for the man of practical wisdom.

THE RELATION BETWEEN EXCELLENCE OF CHARACTER AND WISDOM

Aristotle certainly says that desire, whether rational wish, or appetite, is for the end; if we adhere to the traditional translation, he also says that practical wisdom is concerned with the means to that end. Thus, Ross's translation at 1144a 7–9 reads: 'For virtue makes us aim at the right mark and practical wisdom makes us take the right means'. Aristotle also certainly holds that reason on its own initiates no changes (1139a 35–36). Now this sounds very like Hume's moral psychology. 'Reason', he says, 'is wholly inactive', and he adds that it 'can have an influence on our conduct only after two ways: either when it excites a passion, by informing us of the existence of something which is a proper object of it; or when it discovers the connection of causes and effects, so as to afford us means of exerting any passion'. So Hume can maintain, in a celebrated sentence, that 'reason is, and ought only to be, the slave of passions'.

If Aristotle does hold this Humean view, why should we not be able to have a wholly excellent character and simply lack all ability to plan and execute so as to achieve our worthy goals, and why should we not be excellent at planning and executing the means to wholly bad ends? If it is simply that we are not permitted to call it practical wisdom unless directed towards a good end, this seems to be a mere verbal convention of no substance. So either Aristotle's insistence on the mutual dependence of excellence of character and practical wisdom is merely trivial, or we have, in the preceding paragraph, been misunderstanding him.

We have, indeed, been misunderstanding him. We have been misled by the expression 'means to an end' and it is quite easy to see that such a confined account of the role of reason that leaves it the sole tasks of discovering facts and means to an end is quite inadequate for Aristotle's needs. Let us substitute for Ross's 'virtue makes us aim at the right mark, and practical wisdom makes us take the right means' an alternative and less misleading translation: 'excellence of character makes the goal right and wisdom that which is related to the goal'. The expression 'that which is related to the goal' covers much more than merely means to an end, as a simple illustration will show. A person, we shall suppose, receives through the post many requests for contributions from a variety of charities, and we shall suppose that he is of a charitable disposition, so that he has a rational wish to achieve the goal of being charitable. To achieve this goal he must determine how much money he can reasonably make available, which of the charities are most worthy of support, whether it is better to give much to a few or less to many, and other similar matters; only when he has done all this can he start deliberating and planning the means – shall he send a cheque, cash or a postal order, by post or by hand, and so on. It is quite clear that thought is required to settle all these previous issues and not merely to choose the means. Character may make us wish to be generous, but it cannot decide on its own that the generous thing in the circumstances is, say, to give £5 to the local cats' home. Reason is needed to give a determinate form to our goals and this is not mere means finding.

So how could we display a settled mean disposition to action, which is to be of good character, if we had not the wisdom to determine just what action is appropriate in the circumstances on each occasion? And how could we determine the precise form of plan and execute actions which we had no desire of any sort to perform? Without wisdom, excellence of character would be like a man groping in the dark and not knowing where to go; without the desires of an excellent character, wisdom would have nothing to do. Aristotle says: 'If it is a mark of the wise to have deliberated well, good deliberation will be correctness regarding what conduces to the end, of which practical wisdom is a correct conception' (1142b 31–33). Until one has that correct conception, there is no scope for deliberation.

Once we have grasped the intimate relation that Aristotle perceives between character and reason we shall not be surprised when we find him saying that it is impossible to have excellence of character without practical wisdom or practical wisdom without excellence of character (1144b 30–32). The Humean doctrine that reason provides a knowledge of facts, faced with which we feel a passion, and then merely tells us how to achieve the satisfaction of that passion might seem to have some plausibility with regard to the simpler appetites; but this view is surely too naive to account for the goals we have as rational beings with rational wishes. Right or wrong, Aristotle has at least aimed to do justice to the more complex interrelationship between our desires and capacity for thought.

RULES OF CONDUCT

Having noted Aristotle's accounts of the role of reason in action and the nature of practical wisdom, we might still be inclined to hanker after an answer to that opening question at the beginning of Book VI, especially if we read it in a translation like that of Ross, which reads: 'since . . . the intermediate is determined by the dictates of the right rule, let us discuss the nature of these dictates' (1138b 20). But this is to make the opening of the chapter more misleading than is necessary. A more literal translation of that passage would be: 'since . . . the intermediate is as the right rule (right reason) says, let us examine that'; Aristotle is clearly saying that he is to examine how the intermediate, or mean, is to be determined, but not at all clearly that the answer is to consist in a set of rules. Moreover, he has repeatedly told us that the action will exhibit the excellent or intermediate character has to be decided with reference to a number of variables, such as time, place, persons and goals (1106b 21), and that in particular circumstances there is no general rule by which we can decide. 'Judgement is in perception' (1109b 23) – that is, one can decide only when faced with the concrete situation. No simple rule would be adequate to deal with the complexities of real life.

Given these facts, one cannot expect Aristotle to produce decision procedures for action on every conceivable occasion. Of course, there are important general principles to be discovered and applied by the practically wise man; the whole of the *Nicomachean Ethics* is devoted to determining some of the most ultimate of these principles, such as those that tell us what activities are most worth pursuing in the quest for eudaemonia. But these are not principles by which the mean can be determined on particular occasions. Aristotle does also mention from time to time, for illustrative purposes, various rather trivial principles that are known to the wise man, such as that dry foods are good for man (1147a 5–6). Now he would, no doubt, accept that there are less trivial general principles that guide the practically wise man. He would probably agree that the good man will, when anger is justified with some incompetent organization direct it at the man at the top and not at a subordinate. Obviously, there are many such principles that are known quite widely, but they do not obviate the need for a final judgement, in the light of all the facts, which does not follow automatically from any simple principle or principles.

In this connection a passage at 1144b 26–28 is important: 'An excellent character is not one that merely is (incidentally) in accord with right reason but one that cooperates with right reason. Practical wisdom is right reason in such matters'. So right reason is not some rule, or set of rules, known to the practically wise but is practical wisdom itself. Aristotle holds that an excellent character has to be guided by experience combined with deliberative and executive skills, and it must be aided by a capacity to judge how to act properly in various situations, a capacity which has to be developed in a good education. In early life one's elders must tell one how to act in various situations and, if they are good educators and tell us aright, one will acquire for oneself this capacity for good judgement. There will still be the final principle that one should always act in a way that promotes eudaemonia, but Aristotle is not under the illusion that this on its own can give guidance in practical situations.

So, if we understand the first section of Book VI as proposing merely an account of the rational elements involved in action, that it is right reason not right rules that he is concerned with, Aristotle has given us an answer; but if we regard that section as proposing to give us rules of conduct that will tell us how on each occasion to determine the mean, we shall, very properly and quite inevitably, be disappointed.

REASON AND EUDAEMONIA

In Chapters 12 and 13 of Book VI Aristotle raises questions about the value of both theoretical and practical wisdom. His method, common to all his works, is to raise difficulties and then solve them. He produces arguments to show that both are valueless. Thus, theoretical wisdom is concerned only with the unchanging world of what is necessarily so and therefore gives no knowledge of any use in the world of change in which we live, and so cannot aid us in the search for eudaemonia. (1143b 18–20). Aristotle's answer to this is that since wisdom is an excellence it must be of value. But its value is not as a means to producing eudaemonia; 'it creates eudaemonia, not as medicine creates health, but as health creates health. For it is a part of total excellence and its possession makes a person *eudaemon*' (1144a 3–6). This is a passage that makes crystal clear what has been already pointed out, that for Aristotle eudaemonia is not something separate and distinct from such excellences as wisdom, but this and other excellences are constituents in it. They make up eudaemonia, not in the way that a baker makes up bread, but in the way that flour, water, yeast and salt make up bread.

To the contention that practical wisdom is useless, since what matters is that we should act properly, not that we should have an understanding of how to act properly, Aristotle makes the important, if obvious, retort that, apart from being an excellence and therefore of value in itself, what makes a character excellent and an excellence is that the agent does not merely do what is proper, but does it because it is proper. It is intention that matters and without understanding intent must be imperfect; one can act justly without being just, and so with the other particular excellences. Both character and understanding are necessary for choice.

Finally, in reading Chapters 12 and 13 we cannot but see that Aristotle is already assuming the conclusion, formally arrived at only in Book X, that theoretical wisdom is the most important element in eudaemonia. Thus, one of his initial problems is that if practical wisdom controls our lives it must control the exercise of theoretical wisdom 'although it is inferior to theoretical wisdom' (1143b 34). Aristotle's answer to this is that practical wisdom controls theoretical wisdom only as medicine controls health, as an aid not as a superior. One ancient commentator suggested the analogy of the control of a master's life by his administrative servants. But Aristotle says this only after he has said that practical wisdom is also of value in itself. Aristotle's more and more frequent emphasis on theory as he goes on must not make us forget that he has already emphasized the importance of many other constituents in eudaemonia.

7

Strength and Weakness of Will

By the end of Book VI Aristotle has completed his account of the excellences, both of character and of intellect. But, as we have already noted, there are other possibilities besides having a good or bad character. At the beginning of Book VII of the *Nicomachean Ethics* Aristotle lists three pairs of contrary states of character:

Heroic excellence	Beastliness
Excellence	Badness
Strength of will	Weakness of will

In order of merit, heroic excellence comes first, followed by ordinary excellence, strength of will, weakness of will, badness and beastliness. The first three are good in descending order of merit, the last three, in different degrees, bad. It is strength and weakness of will that we are now to consider. These states are sometimes called 'continence' and 'incontinence' by commentators and weakness is sometimes called *acrasia*, which is simply a transliteration of Aristotle's term in Greek. None of these terms is entirely satisfactory; the reader may prefer to consider 'self-control' and 'lack of self-control'; no English term quite coincides with what Aristotle has in mind. Aristotle's discussion is an early contribution to a debate which continues in lively fashion in our own times.

First, we must get clear why philosophers have found the topic of weakness of will so important and so difficult. The difficulty arises from a fundamental belief that men always desire above all else their own well being or eudaemonia; that a man should deliberately damage himself, not in a limited way for a more important end but absolutely, has seemed to be a psychological impossibility. This being so, it would seem that, if a person knows that acting in a certain way will best promote his wellbeing, he will inevitably so act. But we all of us, in eating, drinking, drug taking and in a thousand other ways, do seem frequently to act against what we know to be our best interests. The problem, typical in philosophy, is how to reconcile these two beliefs, or modify them to make them compatible.

All ancient philosophers and many modern ones have subscribed to the view that men desire above all their own wellbeing. Socrates, convinced of this, pronounced his famous paradox: 'Nobody makes mistakes intentionally'. To go against what one desires most must be a mistake. He who acts against his own highest interest must be acting in ignorance of what is in his interest and contrary to his true intention, which must be to promote his good. So, as Aristotle says, Socrates solved the problem by denying that there was any such phenomenon as weakness of will (1145b 25–26).

Aristotle comments that 'this view is obviously incompatible with the apparent facts' (1145b 27–28). But, since he believes that men desire eudaemonia above all things, he cannot simply say that men knowingly and intentionally act contrary to their eudaemonia. So he has either to accept two apparently contradictory statements:

1 Men always aim at what they know to be in their best interest
2 Men often act in a way that they know to be contrary to their best interest

or else he must abandon one of them, or else he must somehow remove the apparent contradiction. His aim will be to remove the apparent contradiction by making a distinction between different kinds of knowledge. He will try to show that the knowledge present according to statement 2 is not the knowledge referred to in statement 1. In this way he will remove the difficulty. In a memorable passage, that might have been written by a modern analytic philosopher, he writes: 'Here, as elsewhere, we must state the apparent facts and, having raised the difficulties, we must preferably establish all received opinions about these states, or, if not all, the majority and the most important. For if we remove the difficulties and received opinions survive, that is sufficient to establish them' (1145b 8). He later adds that 'the removal of a puzzle is a discovery' (1146b 8).

So, at the beginning of Book VII Chapter 2, he states the first and central puzzle in this way: 'One might raise the problem about the sort of correct conception one has when displaying weak will' (1145b 21–22). Some translations incorrectly put the problem as being how a man can display weak will when he has a correct conception, but this is wrong. The problem is about what sort of knowledge he can have, given that he cannot be allowed to have the full and clear correct conception which will always prevail over appetite. After listing a number of other problems about the strong and the weak will, Aristotle discusses the first and main problem in Chapter 3: does the weak-willed man know what he ought to do, and, if so, what sort of knowledge does he have?

The phenomenon of weakness of will occurs, he says, when there is a conflict between choice, based on rational wish, and appetite (which, we know, is by definition always for pleasure). There is no conflict for the bad man; he chooses deliberately to follow his appetite. The weak-willed man chooses to act for the good but acts in accord with his appetite for the immediately pleasant (1146b 20–24).

Aristotle first considers a proposed solution that claims that the weak-willed man does not act against knowledge of what is best, but only against belief. But he rejects this at once. Belief can be as confident and unquestioned as true knowledge, and it is not only against tentative beliefs that appetite prevails. There is no way out here.

Aristotle turns at once to distinguishing different senses of 'know'. He first makes two distinctions that will not themselves provide a solution to the problem but are necessary preliminaries to a solution. Commentators have not always seen that these are preliminary, but it is clear that neither makes any reference, or needs any reference, to appetite; they distinguish less than full cases of knowledge, but appetite is no more inevitably involved in them than ignorance or faulty memory. The first of these preliminary distinctions is between merely having some piece of knowledge and making use of it; there is no problem of weak will if a man fails to act for the best because he fails to call to mind some knowledge that he possesses (1146b 31–35). The second preliminary distinction is between types of thing known; there is a great difference between knowledge of general principles and knowledge of particular facts; for example, a man may know such general truths as that dry foods are good for men and that chicken is a dry food; but if he does not call to mind, or if he simply does not know, that the poussin listed on the menu or the stuff offered to him on a plate is chicken, he may fail to choose it. Once again, we here have obviously no solution to the problem of weak will, but Aristotle needs the distinction between ignorance of general truths and ignorance of particular facts for his solution.

At 1147a 10 we come to the distinction that Aristotle does believe to be crucial. Our first preliminary distinction was between having and using knowledge; we must now make a distinction between two ways in which we may have, but not use, knowledge. There is the ordinary sort of having but not using that could be illustrated by the fact that the reader probably knows that Germany is in Europe but, equally probably, has not used this knowledge, not called it to mind, in the past five minutes. But there is a kind of having and yet not fully having that is instantiated by the drunk, the sleeper and the madman; while drunk, asleep or mad a man cannot recall the knowledge he has and can use when sober, awake, or sane. Strong appetite, Aristotle tells us, can reduce one to the state of the madman or the drunk. 'It is clear that we must say that the weak willed are like these people' (1147a 17–18).

So now we have the first part of Aristotle's solution to the problem of what sort of knowledge the weak-willed man has. Based on the first of his preliminary distinctions between having and using knowledge, he has introduced a distinction between two sorts of having, such that the weak-willed man has the knowledge at the time of action only in a weak sense, like a man who is drunk. True, he may be able to speak as though he both had and used the knowledge; but in so speaking he will be like a drunk man reciting proofs or verses from the philosophical poems of Empedocles without really grasping the import of his words, or an actor who just recites his part (1147a 20–24).

This is the first part of Aristotle's solution to the problem of weakness of will. But there remains the question just what the weak-willed man fails to recall or understand while in the grip of appetite for some pleasure. His lack of awareness is highly selective; there is no reason to doubt that he knows very clearly that what he is tempted to do is pleasant, for example. Aristotle sets out to answer this question in a very elliptical and much discussed passage from 1147a 24–1147b 18. There is much disagreement about the inevitably somewhat conjectural interpretation of this passage and the reader is hereby warned to examine the interpretation proposed here with his critical faculties fully alert and Aristotle's text before him.

Aristotle explains the situation with an illustration which should call to mind the second of the preliminary distinctions he has recently made. Someone is aware that all sweet things are pleasant and that something before him is sweet; then, if he can, and there is nothing to stop him, he will indulge his appetite. But there might be any number of things that would tend to stop him even if he could indulge; he might be on a diet, or the sweet thing might be somebody else's property, or he might think that sweet things are bad for the health, for example. We constantly have reasons for acting in a certain way, but do not do so because we have still better reasons for acting otherwise. Such a good or better reason would effectively restrain the good or the strong-willed man, but would not stop the weak-willed man, if he were in the grip of an unruly appetite. The weak-willed man fully understands the argument that favours indulgence: 'all sweet things are pleasant, this is sweet and, therefore, pleasant, and so should be tasted'; such an argument is technically called a practical syllogism. But there is also an argument, another practical syllogism, against tasting that will influence the strong-willed man. Aristotle does not give us the full illustr-

ation, merely saying that there will be a universal premiss
stopping him from tasting; so let us suppose it to be: 'sweet
things are bad for the health of men'; then, on the model of the
second preliminary distinction, the argument against tasting will
run somewhat as follows: 'Sweet things are bad for men's health;
chocolate éclairs are sweet things; I am a man and this is a
chocolate éclair; so this would be bad for my health and I should
not taste it'.

The element that the weak-willed man, overcome temporarily
by his appetite, will not fully have and use is, Aristotle tells us,
the final premiss, and this is, if our interpretation is correct, that
the éclair is bad for the health, leading directly to the conclusion
that he should not taste it. This is, as in the syllogism given in
the second preliminary distinction, a premiss about particular
fact. Aristotle explicitly says that weakness of will does not
destroy one's understanding of the universal premiss; so it will
not destroy the knowledge that sweet things are bad for the
health. Nor, clearly, can it destroy the knowledge that chocolate
éclairs are sweet and that this is an éclair, for both of these facts
are part of the considerations that give the weak-willed man his
appetite to taste. He wants to taste because he knows full well
that éclairs are sweet and that this is an éclair. What he fails to
actuate, in the grip of his appetite, is the knowledge that this
now is bad for him, something he knows in a way and knows
fully when not in the grip of appetite. Perhaps the overweight
man, as he takes the éclair and bites into it, will say, 'I should
not be eating this'; but, if he does, he will not fully realize the
import of what he says. If he did, he would not take the éclair.
He might just as well be reciting Empedoclean verses.

So Aristotle claims that he can have it both ways. He can deny
the Socratic paradox: 'there is no such a state as weakness of will',
and he has explained how it happens. But the opinions of the
wise and common sense must be vindicated when possible, and
Aristotle can claim that the most important of Socrates' conten-
tions can be preserved. It is not true universal knowledge that is
overcome by pleasure in weakness of will, but the 'judgment of
preception' that the immediate situation falls under the universal. None but the bad man acts against the best with full

knowledge, but the common-sense view that there is such a thing as weak will is preserved since the weak-willed man acts against knowledge of a sort, knowledge that will be fully actualized when the appetite is absent and will lead to regret. As Aristotle says later:

> There is a person who departs from right reason because of his emotion, whom the emotion forces not to act according to right reason but does not force to be the sort of person who believes that it is proper to pursue such pleasures without restraint. This is the weak-willed man, who is better than the intemperate man and not simply bad; for the most valuable element, the basic premiss, is preserved. (1151a 20–26)

There are other matters concerning weakness and strength of will that Aristotle discusses before turning to the topic of pleasure. Thus, endurance of distress or pain is distinguished from strength to resist the temptations of pleasure; also, brutishness, the condition of the person who through congenital defect, disease or ill-treatment becomes perverted in a way that makes him subhuman and not subject to normal moral appraisal, is distinguished from simple badness of character. But these topics are clearly and well discussed in Aristotle's text and need no commentary. But there are certain matters connecting the topic of weakness of will with the impending discussion of pleasure that need to be noted.

In Book VII Chapter 4 Aristotle tells us that the Greek term here translated as 'weak-willed' can be applied without qualification only in the field wherein temperance is the excellence – such matters as the pleasures of eating, drinking and sex. People who display the same lack of self-control with regard to other emotions can be said to be weak-willed only with an added qualification. In stilted translationese we must say 'weak-willed with regard to anger (gain, honour, etc.)' More naturally we should say, for example, that a person cannot control his temper, cannot resist a quick profit and the like. So certain pleasures are marked off as being within the sphere of temperance and as being the only ones that can be said, when they overcome us, to involve weakness of will without qualification. This, of course, is not true with regard to the English term 'weak-willed', but that is merely a defect of our translation, for what Aristotle says is certainly true of the Greek term as usually employed.

But these points raise numerous problems to which we need an answer. Here are some of them. Why did the Greeks single out certain pleasures in this way, those that Aristotle says are primarily related to eating, drinking and sex, excluding all the other pleasures that all normal people seek and enjoy? Are such pleasures as those of active sports, walking, swimming and gardening not bodily pleasures? If they are not, why are they not? If they are, why are they not treated as being in the field of temperance? Are these distinctions arbitrary, or is there good reason for them? These are among the problems that we must hope will be resolved by Aristotle's examination of pleasure, if we are to feel satisfied that we understand Aristotle's views on weakness of will. We need to have a more explicit understanding of the concept of pleasure and Aristotle does proceed immediately to discuss that concept. His two discussions of pleasure do not explicitly answer the questions we have raised, but answers to them can be gathered from what he has to say on the topic.

8

Pleasure

There are two discussions of pleasure in the *Nicomachean Ethics*, neither of which refers to or shows any awareness of the other. One is in Book VII, Chapters 11–14, the other in Book X, Chapters 1–5. In certain respects they are complementary; thus, only Book VII discusses arguments directed to show that all, or some, pleasures are bad in themselves; only Book X discusses the claim that pleasure is the sole or supreme good. But both discuss the nature of pleasure and give what at first sight seems to be different answers. There can be little doubt that both discussions are genuine writings of Aristotle and little doubt also that they cannot have been designed as part of a single work. We may reasonably guess that pious editors, unwilling to lose either, cobbled them into the same work in a rather clumsy fashion. Each discussion does, in fact, occur quite naturally in its context. In Book VII Aristotle has been examining the way that pleasure, or the desire for it, can lead the weak willed astray, so that it is perfectly natural to go on to discuss pleasure and natural to examine the suggestion that pleasure is bad. In Book X, where Aristotle is about to offer his final sketch of the nature of eudaemonia, it is natural that the claim of pleasure to be the highest good and its relation to other activities constitutive of eudaemonia should receive close attention.

There were philosophers of Plato's school who, unlike Plato himself, held that all pleasure was wholly bad, and also some who held that at least the bodily pleasures were bad. Even today the expression 'a life of pleasure' can be used with disparaging overtones. Aristotle's rebuttal of such views is crushing. We need not follow his arguments in detail, but should note two of them.

Against those who hold that all pleasure is bad on the ground that it interferes with more important things, he points out that the pleasure of thinking, 'or the pleasure of doing anything else' does not interfere with what one is doing, but rather enhances it (1153a 20–23). It is 'foreign pleasures' that impede activities. As he says later on (1175b 3–5), a music lover may have difficulty in attending to an argument when he hears music. But people who enjoy, say, mathematics, are more likely to work with concentration and absorption than those who do not. The pleasure that one gets from the activity itself he calls the proper pleasure of that activity. Proper pleasures enhance, foreign pleasures make laborious, their activity. One can also speak of the 'proper pain' of an activity, which is the dislike of the activity that, like a foreign pleasure, can make it laborious.

Aristotle thinks that those who have held all pleasure to be bad have done so because they have equated pleasure with the bodily pleasures. When people speak of pleasure without qualification they usually mean just the bodily pleasures. 'The bodily pleasures have appropriated the name both because we very often steer towards them and because everyone participates in them' (1153b 3–5). But, with his normal common sense, he points out that even the attack on bodily pleasures is mistaken. Eating, drinking and sex are necessary parts of human life and are naturally pleasant. Excessive indulgence is what is bad, not the pleasure itself. The *eudaemon* man needs food and drink and their pleasures and in general pleasant circumstances of life. To say that one can be *eudaemon* even under torture or in great misfortune, provided one is good, is rubbish (1153b 17–21).

We need not follow Aristotle through all the details of his defence of pleasure. But two points emerge from this defence that are important for Aristotle's positive views. The first is that pleasure is an activity and not a process, the second that it is an unimpeded activity (e.g., 1153b 17–21). These two points need explanation.

PROCESS AND ACTIVITY

The distinction between process and activity is one that Aristotle makes in a number of different contexts. He offers several criteria for distinguishing between them which seem to be closely interrelated. The main sources for the distinction are *Metaphysics*, 1048b 18–35 and the first four chapters of Book X of the *Nicomachean Ethics*. Behind the distinction lies a still more fundamental distinction between what is merely potential and what is actual; thus a seed is actually a seed but only potentially a plant. But within the actual in this wide sense he distinguishes what is commonly translated 'activity' from process or change. Some translators use the terms 'activity' and 'motion', but this involves calling such processes as tomato ripening or a man growing old a motion, which is odder than is necessary. It must be admitted that 'activity' cannot be used truly idiomatically, but nobody has yet suggested an improvement.

The three main criteria for distinguishing activity from process are: 1 If 'A is X-ing' entails 'A has X-ed' then X-ing is an activity; if 'A is X-ing' is incompatible with 'A has X-ed' then X-ing is a process. Thus, if it be true that Tom is looking at a temple, then it is true that Tom has looked at a temple; but if Tom is building a temple he cannot have built it. So looking at something is an activity, building something is a process. 2 An activity may last for a period of time but does not take time, whereas a process takes time. Thus, one may look at a temple for a long time, but it does not make sense to ask how long it takes to look at it; but it does make sense to ask how long it takes to inspect it throughly or to build it. So, once again, looking at something is an activity, but inspecting it or building it is a process. 3 An activity is complete in itself at any time and logically can go on indefinitely, whereas a process is essentially incomplete all the time that it is going on and, when completed, must terminate. Aristotle sometimes puts this point by saying that an activity has its end in itself while a process has an end apart from itself with, as we shall see, unfortunate results. According to this criterion, if Tom is looking at a temple, he is as much looking at it at the first instant he does so as at any other time, the looking does not become more complete; also he logically, though not in practice, could go on looking at it for ever. But if he is building a temple, his building is incomplete at any time but grows nearer to completion, and when the temple is built, is complete, he is no longer building it. So, once again, looking at something is an activity, building is a process.

We must note that if we say that Tom's looking at a temple is complete at any time, we must mean that Tom is wholly looking at it at any time, not that he is at any time looking at the whole temple. Similarly listening to a symphony is an activity because one is wholly listening at any time; one is obviously not listening to the whole symphony at any time. So in the sense in which 'Tom is listening to a symphony' entails 'Tom has listened to a symphony', it clearly does not entail that he has listened to a whole symphony, but only that at some time 'he is listening to a symphony' has been true. Perhaps listening is ambiguously an activity or a process as we use the term; thus, in response to the question: 'Have you ever listened to Beethoven's 5th?' someone who has listened only to a portion of it may answer equally: 'Yes, but not to all of it', or 'No, only to part of it'.

A warning is necessary to anyone who proposes to follow up this distinction in Aristotle's text. There he uses what translators not unnaturally call 'walking' as a stock example of a process. But walking seems to satisfy all the criteria for being an activity. A solution to this difficulty is offered by *Rhetoric* 1405a 5–7, where the verb is said to be synonymous with a verb whose meaning is 'to journey on foot'. Making a journey, whether on foot or not, is certainly a process. The Greeks had another word for just going for a walk, or walking about without a destination, which is an activity; it is a word from which 'peripatetic' is derived, which refers to people who, like Aristotle, walk about while talking philosophy.

This Aristotelian distinction between activity and process is not without difficulties, well ventilated by scholars, but is clear enough for our purposes. It is surely clear that taking pleasure in, or enjoying, something is an activity and not a process. If Tom is enjoying looking at a temple, then he henceforth has enjoyed looking at it, logically he can go on enjoying it for ever, and it does not take time to enjoy it, even if he takes some time to start to enjoy it. But though it is obviously true that enjoyment of anything is an activity and not a process, one may well wonder why Aristotle so frequently asserts that enjoyment is an activity and not a process, and thinks it so important, and it is to that question that we must now address ourselves.

Taking hunger and thirst as paradigm cases of distressing situations and generalizing from them, Greek physicians had come to the conclusion that where there was pain there was a deficiency of something necessary for bodily wellbeing. In the paradigm cases the deficiencies were obviously of food and drink. The process of restoration, of refilling, that ended the deficiency was inherently pleasant. These medical theories encouraged the philosophical view that Aristotle attacks in Chapter 12 of Book VII, that pleasure is a perceived process of restoration. Essentially his reply there is that true and lasting pleasures, such as theoretical contemplation (1153a 1), unlike those presupposing some bad state from which to start, such as those of eating and drinking, are not concerned with restoring any deficiency, and that we should regard pleasure as the unimpeded activity of the good state, not as 'a process of becoming from a bad state' (1153a 13–15). Thus the pleasure of contemplation will derive from the contemplator's being in good health, not tired, and the like.

So the first part of the answer to the question why Aristotle so strongly insists on the activity-process distinction is that the view that pleasure is a process was associated with a view of pleasure that sees it as a mere repair of bodily functions. Aristotle has insisted that the activities of the man of good character are naturally pleasant, and will argue for the importance of contemplation in life partly on the ground that its pleasures do not presuppose a preceding distress. This requires a view of pleasure that does not link it necessarily with any sort of change.

Aristotle's other reason for denying that pleasure is a process is less satisfactory, but plays an important role in his views. We have seen that there is one criterion for distinguishing activity from process that is sometimes stated in the form 'activity has its end in itself, process has an end outside itself'. We must now distinguish two different meanings that may be given to this formulation of the criterion. We may mean that activities are what they are solely in virtue of their internal nature, whereas processes are identified as what they are in virtue of what will count as their completion. Thus, looking at a temple is what it is because of what is going on at that time. But clearing sites, carrying bricks around and the like are not from their internal nature temple-building; they are elements in temple-building only if they are directed towards a final state which is a temple having been built. On this interpretation the criterion is quite clear and satisfactory.

But, if we turn back to the very beginning of the Nicomachean Ethics, we find a different interpretation of the activity-process distinction, not yet explicitly stated, being presupposed. Having distinguished between ends that are the activity itself and ends that are beyond the activity (1094a 4-5), he states that the external ends are more valuable than the actions that bring them about. As this and subsequent remarks show, Aristotle holds that activities in the narrow sense are valuable in themselves whereas processes are pursued only for the sake of their results or products. He can produce plausible examples from manufacturing to back up this claim. But, while it may be a statistical truth that we make things only for the sake of the end product, it is by no means universally true. It is not usually the case that people solve crossword puzzles solely for the pleasure of contemplating the finished product or for putting it to some use; they do not prove theorems in mathematics purely in order to have theorems, nor build sand castles on the beach in order to possess or use sand castles. There are many processes where the chase is the thing and the goal, once reached, relatively unimportant. In principle, there is no process that people (if eccentric enough) might not carry out for its own sake, because they enjoy carrying it out. In general Aristotle has a low view of the exercise of a craft, art or skill on the ground that one does not make a thing for the sake of the making, but in order to possess the thing. This is clear from the discussion of skills in Book VI, Chapter 4 and elsewhere. But he is not entitled to draw this conclusion from the fact that a case of making is defined in terms of the envisaged end product, and any survey shows that much making is undertaken for its own sake, at least in part.

We must conclude that Aristotle's use of the distinction between activity and process in order to distinguish the inherently pleasurable from that which is done merely for the sake of some end product or external goal is a mistake. It is a mistake that will have, as we shall increasingly see, serious consequences.

ARISTOTLE'S POSITIVE ACCOUNT OF PLEASURE

When Aristotle says that pleasure or enjoyment is an unimpeded activity of that which is in a good state (1153a 13-15), he does not surely mean that enjoyment is a separate activity that goes on in parallel with the activity that one enjoys. Thus, he does not mean that the player of a round of golf finds himself simultaneously playing a round of golf, impeded in this activity, no doubt, by bunkers and the like, and also indulging in an activity of enjoyment, this time unimpeded. He should be taken to mean that the activity of playing golf, or whatever, has the characteristic of being enjoyable precisely if it is not impeded by such impediments as desires to do something else instead, bad form and the like. If we so interpret him, the view he puts forward in Book VII, while verbally different, is not seriously at variance with what he has to say in Book X, and it is to the more systematic account of pleasure in that book that we shall now turn. 'Pleasure is an unimpeded activity' will be understood to mean that any activity in which we engage will be pleasant if it is not impeded by such relevant impediments as tiredness, distractions and the like. This is not seriously different from saying that pleasure is a certain perfection or completion of an activity, as Aristotle says in Book X.

Pleasure, like sight, Aristotle holds, is an activity, not a process. Perception, of which sight is an example, thought and contemplation have objects. When the perception or thought is high grade and its object is worthwhile, then the perception, thought or contemplation is enjoyable or pleasant. The higher grade the perception or thought, and the more valuable its object, the more pleasant and more perfect is the activity. But excellence of the perception or thought and of its object make the activity perfect in a way different from that in which enjoyment perfects it. The former constitute its perfection whereas the enjoyment is an additional perfection. Commentators are not agreed about how this additional or supervenient perfection is to be understood, but I think it is the frictionless zest with which the activity will be performed when it is enjoyed. This is very like the notion of the activity being unimpeded. When, through illness or tiredness, the activity is impaired, so is the enjoyment of it. Again, novelty commands effortless attention and, therefore, enjoyment, but, when novelty wears off, attention is apt to wander and enjoyment to wane. So activity and life itself are bound up with enjoyment: there is no pleasure without activity enjoyed, and enjoyment is the mark of activity at peak performance.

Different activities are differently enjoyable (1175a 21). Just as perception and thought are different species of activity, so the pleasures of perception are different in species from those of thought. Every activity has its own 'proper' or special pleasure; one could not chance to get the pleasure of, say, reading poetry from stamp collecting. The pleasure proper to an activity promotes that activity, whereas the enjoyment of something else, what Aristotle calls 'a foreign pleasure', impedes it. (We should notice the use here of the word 'impede' and connect its use with the expression 'unimpeded activity' in Book VII). If we are doing two things at once, the more enjoyable gets in the way of the other. So when we enjoy something very much we do not do anything else at the same time; we eat sweets at the theatre, Aristotle observes, only when we are not greatly enjoying the play (1175b 12–13). So if two pleasures conflict, rather than reinforcing each other, they must be different. In general, the enjoyment of an activity and the activity itself are so bound up with one another that 'it might be debated whether the activity is the same thing as the pleasure' (1175b 33).

In marked contrast to this final emphatic statement of the intimate connection between an activity and its pleasure, it has been commonplace in the history of philosophy to regard the pleasure gained from an activity as some sort of feeling or sensation resulting from the activity. This pleasure is an undifferentiated something, quantities of which can be added together and weighed against other parcels of the same commodity.

Psychological hedonists have typically assumed this analysis and concluded from it that mankind has only one goal of action called 'pleasure', other activities differing from each other in worth only according to their capacity to produce this indifferentiated experience. Sometimes their opponents have seemed to think that to reject psychological hedonism they must say that we do not do things for pleasure but for their own sake, thus consenting to the analysis; they, too, take the pleasure of an activity to be a feeling resulting from it, but claim that the pleasure is a mere bonus resulting from gaining what one wants rather than the end for the sake of which the activity was performed. But for Aristotle the enjoyment of an activity is not a result of it but something barely distinguishable from the activity itself; for him, doing a thing for the sheer pleasure of doing it is doing it for its own sake.

Perhaps it is easy to see the attractiveness of this position in the case of such intellectual pleasures as solving a mathematical problem. If someone works away at it oblivious of his surroundings and his own bodily condition, totally unwilling to be distracted from it and without ulterior motive, such as payment, how could it be denied that he is enjoying it? But what of the bodily pleasures? It is clear that in Book X Aristotle wishes to give the same general account of them as of purely intellectual pleasures. Widely construed, bodily pleasures include all activities that involve the use of any of our bodily organs and limbs. They include the enjoyment of colours and shapes and pictures (sight), of music (hearing) and the scent of flowers (smell). Thus to enjoy music is to listen to it effortlessly, not willing to be distracted and so on. But the objects of taste and touch have, as we have noted, a special position among bodily pleasures in this wide sense. They are the sole sphere of temperance and the only ones regarding which we can be said to be weak-willed without qualification. Usually, when Aristotle speaks of bodily pleasures he seems to have these pleasures of taste and touch solely in mind (e.g., at 1104b 5, 1153b 33, 1154a 8, 1154a 26 and 1177a 7). We still have to see what is so special about them.

We have seen that Aristotle allots a special position to the objects of touch and taste and makes little effort to distinguish between them. In an important passage he makes it clear that touch is the true sphere of temperance and taste comes in only as a kind of touch: 'They [the intemperate] seem to make little use of taste. For to taste belongs the judgment of flavours, as is done by wine tasters and cooks. But it is not these that people enjoy, intemperate ones at any rate, but the experience which is all a matter of touch, whether in the field of food or drink or sex' (1118a 26–33). Here Aristotle is on the brink of making a distinction far more important than his general distinction of the enjoyment of perceptual and intellectual activities. We must now turn our attention to this distinction that he never quite makes clear, even to himself, but which he obviously needs.

Aristotle's general account of pleasure or enjoyment of activity is surely persuasive, in contrast to those accounts that make such enjoyment the obtaining of pleasant experiences produced by the activity. But, surely, there is such a thing as gaining pleasant experiences as a result of an activity, even if this is not what it is to enjoy that activity. While solving a mathematical problem one may be so absorbed in it that one does not notice one's feelings; but, when one has solved it, might one not feel a most exhilarating feeling of pleasure as a result of solving it? Swimming, however enjoyable itself, may also on a hot day produce an agreeable sense of coolness and invigoration. But Aristotle treats all pleasures, including all bodily pleasures, as being the enjoyment of activities of thought or sense perception. The latter may be less clear or pure than those of intellectual activity, and may arise from painful conditions such as thirst, but he seems to think that they can be subsumed without remainder under the same general analysis.

But it is clear that the distress caused by thirst, which is alleged to be the opposite of the pleasure of drinking, is not like the disagreeableness that some find in doing geometry, which is the opposite of finding geometry enjoyable. When we find geometry disagreeable, on Aristotle's analysis, we tend to avoid geometry and are distracted from it with the greatest of ease. But he cannot claim that the distress caused by thirst is such that we find it hard to attend to it and are easily distracted from it. Again, geometry has both its 'proper' pleasure and its 'proper' distress or pain, but we do not hear of a proper pain of drinking or proper pleasure of thirst. The reason for these facts is clear: the pangs of thirst are unpleasant sensations caused by thirst and not the unwelcomeness of thirst, and the pleasure of drinking is not the frictionless ingestion of liquid but a pleasant sensation caused by drinking when thirsty.

Certainly Aristotle's account of enjoyment can be applied to activities essentially involving even the sense of touch. One may, as he points out, be interested in tastes and enjoy tasting things in the same way as an expert cook or connoisseur of wines is likely to be (1118a 28–29). Again, many activities involving other senses, such as looking at pictures and listening to music, are easily subsumed under Aristotle's account. But we should notice that these activities are looking at or watching, listening to, tasting (as in wine tasting) and smelling (sniffing at), not merely seeing, hearing, having a taste in one's mouth or having an odour in one's nostrils.

There could be a parallel enjoyment of the activity of touching, involving such things as the discrimination of textures; the blind sometimes enjoy handling statues in this way. But it is clear that when the intemperate or weak-willed man eats, drinks and indulges in sexual activity to excess he is characterized, not as enjoying these activities, but as performing them in order to produce pleasant sensations. It is the feelings that are enjoyed by the intemperate, not the activities that engender them. But Aristotle fails to make this point explicit in his analysis of pleasure; he persuades himself that the intemperate pleasures are to be distinguished from others because they involve the sense of touch, and thus fails to see that what he needs is a distinction between the enjoyment of activities, whether of touch or other sense or of intellect, as such and the enjoyment of the feelings and sensations that they may produce. There is no activity that might not, in principle, produce pleasant or unpleasant sensations.

So, in conclusion of this discussion, we can now say why Aristotle was right to mark off the pleasures of the intemperate man from the other pleasures that he has been analysing and why it is reasonable to mark off weakness of will without qualification from overindulgence in various activities. They are rightly marked off becaue they are cases of pleasant feeling produced by touch and not this activity itself. Aristotle was often on the verge of seeing this, but instead mistakenly made the distinction as being between the use of the sense of touch and other activities. Philosophers have always been liable to overlook the difference between enjoying an activity and enjoying feelings and sensations and, in general, states of mind and body produced by the activity. But whereas most philosophers have made the mistake of assimilating the enjoyment of an activity to the enjoyment of the states it produces, Aristotle makes the uncommon mistake of treating the enjoyment of produced states as being a special case of enjoyment of activity.

One final word of warning is perhaps advisable. We must not be misled by the word 'activity', which is throughout this discussion being used as a term of art. Aristotle is not committed to the view that one has to be active, on the go, if life is to be pleasant. As the word 'activity' is being used here, lying on the beach and doing nothing is as much a case of activity as anything naturally so called. One does not need to be concentrating hard on lying there for it to be pleasant; just not wanting to get up and do something, not being restless, not noticing the passage of time and the like are enough to make one's inactivity pleasant. The inactivity is clearly an activity in the technical sense since it is not in itself the bringing about of an end product, does not take time, though it may last for a time, and if one is lying on the beach one has lain on the beach. It must also be emphasizd that in denying that the excellence of temperance is concerned with the desire to use the senses of touch and taste and suggesting instead that it is concerned with the desire for the feelings or sensations that are produced by touching and tasting, we have not denied that these pleasures are activities rather than processes. Clearly, if one now is experiencing the taste of garlic, then it immediately becomes true that one has tasted the taste of garlic, one may in principle continue to taste that taste for ever (and almost, in fact, does), and there is no end product the production of which constitutes the experience as tasting garlic.

9

Social Relationships

At the beginning of the *Nicomachean Ethics* (1094a 25-b 4) Aristotle tells us that ethics is a department of the theory of politics; both are concerned with determining the good for man, but ethics considers only the good for man abstracted from the community, whereas politics proper will include the study of civil societies, which also exist for the good for men, in their complete social context. So ethics is the prolegomenon to politics, and the final sentence of the work is: 'So let us begin our discussion' (1181b 22–23). The end of the ethical work is to be regarded as the beginning of politics.

There is a famous remark in the *Politics* (1253a 2), to be found also in almost identical words in the *Nicomachean Ethics* (1169b 18), that (as usually translated) 'Man is naturally a political animal'. What Aristotle means is that it is natural for man to live in organized civil societies. But there are social relationships into which people enter that fall short of being so comprehensive as citizenship, and the eighth and ninth books of the *Nicomachean Ethics* are devoted to examining some of these and considering what place they have in the good life. These books are traditionally said to be on friendship, and Aristotle uses the one word, naturally translated 'friendship', to refer to all these social relationships; but a reading of Aristotle's text soon shows that this title is too narrow to cover all the relationships that Aristotle will discuss.

It would seem that these two books go beyond the bounds of ethics as defined by Aristotle, and they seem to be an editorial

addition, though obviously genuine. Thus Book VII ends its final
discussion of pleasure with the words: 'Finally we shall speak
about friendship' (1154b 34), while Book IX ends the discussion
of friendship with the words: 'We should next discuss pleasure'
(1172a 15); this is surely clumsy stitching together of separate
pieces. Moreover there is no reference to these two books in the
rest of the *Nicomachean Ethics,* and there is only one reference in
them to the rest of the work, at 1170a 25, where Aristotle says
that the nature of distress (pain) will become clearer in what
follows. Theoretically, these books discuss a topic intermediate
between the good of man considered in isolation and that good in
large-scale political organizations, that can better be called the
topic of social relationships within such comprehensive organizations than that of friendship only.

Since the rest of the *Nicomachean Ethics* artificially neglects the
importance of social relationships in the *eudaemon* life, save in a
few casual remarks, we should note the emphasis that Aristotle
puts on the importance of friendship in these books. Nobody, he
tells us, would choose to live without friends, even if he had all
other good things (1155a 5–6); a good man needs friends and it is
a mark of a good man that he can make friends (1155a 27–30).It
is more reasonable to regard Aristotle as systematically treating
man in abstraction from his social relationships in the rest of the
work, rather than to suppose that he has elsewhere forgotten
about the social relationships of life and hastily sets out to remedy
the oversight in these two books.

In Chapter 2 of Book VIII Aristotle repeats his regular view
that there are generically three objects of love and desire, the
pleasant, the good and the useful. In speaking of loving the
useful we are obviously talking traditional translationese; no
doubt it would be better to say that we value it. On this
distinction he bases in Chapter 3 a second between three types of
friendship (in his wide sense). We have relationships with people
because such relationships are useful, such people as those whom
nowadays we might call business associates; with other people
such as bridge partners and witty conversationalists, we form
associations for entertainment and pleasure. These two types of
association, if they are no more than that, do not, like true

friendship, have the person as their object but the utility or pleasure he provides; the association will naturally end as soon as it ceases to serve its purpose.

The third type of association, true friendship, is rare, for it can be only between people both of whom are good and who wish each other well for the other's sake. True friends are, indeed, pleasant and useful to each other, but the friendship does not have pleasure or utility as its object. The other types of association may be between two bad men or between a good and a bad, but, Aristotle holds, true friendship can exist only between good men and equals and must be reciprocal. There can be no one-sided friendships, though there can be one-sided good will or benefit.

There are, however, social relationships, not naturally called friendships, where the parties are unequal in status. Examples are those of father and son, husband and wife, ruler and subject. Many of the details of Aristotle's views on this topic are unlikely to commend themselves to modern readers, who may deny the inequality of status and find the view that in each case the inferior ought to love the superior more than he is loved repulsive. But, even so, Aristotle's insistence that loving is more of the essence of friendship than being loved (1159a 33–35) helps to mitigate his occasionally outdated opinions.

Aristotle interestingly links these unequal relationships with forms of government in the state. He distinguishes three good forms of government, each having its own characteristic perversion, making six in all. Schematically they are.

Good Form	Perversion
Monarchy	Tyranny
Aristocracy	Oligarchy
Timocracy	Democracy

Of these the first two are self-explanatory; timocracy is a form of government in which power is widely and evenly spread between all who satisfy a property qualification, its perversion democracy, being the state where all are equal in authority, whatever their status – something Aristotle regards as not as bad as tyranny or oligarchy, but likely to be disorganized and ill-advised. The wild excesses of the Athenian democracy left the ancient philosophers with a deep suspicion of extreme direct democracy; though Aristotle was not as hostile to it as was Plato, he thought that it gave power without the responsibility to be expected of those with a stake in the country.

Aristotle now finds the following parallels:

> The good relation of father to son is like monarchy; its perversion is tyranny.
> The good relation of husband to wife is like aristocracy; but where the wife is not allowed her proper share of influence and the husband dominates in everything the relationship becomes akin to oligarchy.
> The good relation of brothers is like timocracy; but a household where nobody holds sway is like a democracy.

How far these parallels are accurate and illuminating in detail may be debated; but they form part of Aristotle's general view that a household is a microcosm reflecting the more inclusive relationships holding within a state and exhibiting parallel merits and defects.

The further details of Aristotle's account of the principles governing various types of association, from true friendship to commercial relationships like that of the shoemaker and his customer (1163b 38), need not be further examined here. They are readily comprehensible and vary from the wise and penetrating to those reflecting outdated and unfamiliar social scenes and practices.

FRIENDSHIP AND EGOISM

There remains a crucial problem: in general, the tone of the ethical writings is egocentric. All the ingredients put forward as elements in the good life seem to be advocated as promoting the well being of the agent. This seems true of the excellences of intelligence and character as well as of less central matters such as good looks, good birth and material prosperity. It is no less true because Aristotle clearly despises the self-seeking man in the everyday sense of that term. Yet in his account of true friendship, which he has declared to be an essential element in the good life, Aristotle seems to recognize genuine disinterested love as governing the behaviour of friends. Thus, Chapter 4 of Book IX begins with the emphatic statement that a friend is essentially one who seeks the good of his friend for his friend's sake, as a mother seeks the good and life of her child.

Thus we are faced with a problem. If the good life contains essentially true friendship, and if true friendship contains essentially disinterested care for the interest of the friend, then it would seem that the good life cannot be identified with the life that is most *eudaemon* for him who lives it; but Aristotle has said that the good life is identical with eudaemonia, which is defined as living and faring well. The problem is whether we have here a fundamental contradiction in Aristotle's views, or whether he can reconcile the at first sight irreconcilable. Aristotle is, of course, aware of the problem, and we must see how he sets out to deal with it. His treatment of it is mainly to be found in Chapters 4 and 8 of Book IX.

Aristotle starts by saying that the main features of friendship – disinterested care for welfare and life, and sharing life, interests, joys and griefs – are as much true of a good man's relation to himself as of his relations to his friends. The good man does not regret the life he leads, does not wish to be different and in general regards himself in the way that he is supposed to regard his friends. So if the main features of friendship constitute love of the friend, we must say that the good man loves himself. Aristotle is, of course, aware that self-love is usually a term of abuse: 'People blame those who love themselves most and call them lovers of self as a term of shame . . ., whereas the good man acts for his friend's sake, and sacrifices his own interest' (1168a 29–35). But Aristotle says that this is a misunderstanding. The good man is a lover of self in the good sense, and the wicked man loves himself in the bad sense. This line of thought is interestingly echoed in the eighteenth century by Bishop Butler who, in his sermons preached in the Rolls Chapel, told his fashionable and cynical audience that the trouble with true self-love was that it was too rare, not that it was too common.

What Aristotle now has (1169a 18 ff) to say is crucial and must be quoted at length:

> It is true of the good man that he does much for the sake of his friends and his country, and will die for them if necessary; he will surrender both wealth and honours and generally the goods men fight for, but gaining nobility for himself. For he prefers great pleasure for a short time to enduring slight pleasure, and to live nobly for a year rather then for many years in nondescript fashion, and one fine and great action to many small ones. This presumably happens to those who die for others, for they choose something great and fine for themselves. . . . In all praiseworthy deeds the good man appears to allot to himself the greatest share of nobility. In this way, then, one should be a lover of self, as has been said, but not in the way most people are.

This line of argument, at least at first sight, does not do what is required of it. There is a great difference between a sacrifice for the sake of another, which can be rightly described as fine or noble, and giving up something to another in order to attain the greater good of having achieved something fine and noble. If one makes a sacrifice for another in order to attain a greater good, then it is not true that one has made the sacrifice for the sake of that other. If this line of argument is correct, Aristotle has failed to reconcile his view of friendship as involving disinterested care for the friend's welfare with his general view that men seek what they take to be their highest good.

But we must look carefully at this notion of acting in a certain way 'because it is fine (noble)' or 'for the sake of what is fine (noble)'. Aristotle introduces this notion a number of times in the *Nicomachean Ethics*, particularly in contexts which seem to involve a person in acting against his interests. Thus, he speaks in the present context of sacrifice for a friend for the sake of what is fine and in his discussion of bravery he more than once speaks of the brave man as facing death because it is

fine to do so (e.g., 1115b 5). At 1104b 30–33 he says that there
are three objects of choice, the fine, the useful and the pleasant of
which the opposites respectively are the base, the harmful and the
distressing; this should give us pause, since he constantly says
that the three objects of desire are the good, the useful and the
pleasant, and three opposites, the bad, the harmful and the
distressing; at 1155b18 he has said that the three objects of love
are the good, the useful and the pleasant. At this stage we might
begin to wonder what this term 'fine (noble)' can mean. The
Greek word *kalon*, which is regularly translated as 'fine' or 'noble'
in ethical contexts is also regularly translated 'beautiful' in other
contexts; it is thus used of scenery and people; its opposite,
translated 'base' in ethical contexts, is also the regular word for
what is ugly. In the *Rhetoric* (1366a 33) Aristotle defines the *kalon*
as 'the praiseworthy good in itself' or 'the pleasant because good'.
In the *Topics* (145a 22) he defines it as 'the fitting'. If we attempt
to draw conclusions from these data, it would seem that *kalon* is
either an aesthetic or (in ethical contexts) a quasi-aesthetic term
and that thus 'fine' may well be the best translation to employ. It
would seem that the fine in ethical contexts is opposed to what is
sordid, base mean and thus ugly. It may be bad to rob a bank of
millions, but it will be mean or base to rob a poor old woman of
her pitiful and meagre assets. To eat moderately may be good,
pre-eminent self-sacrifice will be fine. A good man will not be
able to live with himself if he behaves sordidly or meanly, and so
will choose rather to die. So the fine or noble should perhaps be
thought of as this special type of the good that is the opposite of
the mean and base. This interpretation seems to harmonize best
with the definitions of the *Rhetoric* and the *Topics*, since the notion
of the fitting may well have an aesthetic or an ethical tone. The
distinction between what is simply wrong and what is mean,
shabby or base is one which nowadays can still gain sympathetic
understanding.

So, now, if the situation is such that one can save one's friend
only by sacrificing one's own life, and one makes this sacrifice
because one would despise oneself for ever after if one did not, is
one loving one's friend for his own sake or being selfish? One
might reply that unless he were a true friend, and not a mere

business acquaintance or boon companion, there would be nothing sordid in not making the sacrifice, that it is precisely because one values him for his own sake that it would be sordid not to make the sacrifice. In this way we may attempt to claim that Aristotle successfully achieves the reconciliation of his theories of human motivation. If one is asked why one is making a sacrifice for another person and answers: 'I could not live with myself if I did not', is one thereby showing that one does not value that person and his welfare, but only one's own welfare? Why should one not be able to live with oneself if one thus failed unless one did value that person's welfare? Whether this attempt to save Aristotle's argument from the imputation of failure is successful I am not sure, and the reader must decide for himself.

Further discussions follow in Aristotle's text, including a most elaborate chain of argument to show that one cannot have more than a few true friends, something one might accept intuitively without the argument. Most of these are self-explanatory and need no discussion here. But something should be said about the notion of self-sufficiency. It will be remembered that in Book I of the *Nicomachian Ethics* Aristotle had already said that one of the criteria of the *eudaemon* life was that it was self-sufficient; in Book X he is going to tell us that one of the grounds for regarding a life devoted to contemplation as the most *eudaemon* is that it eminently satisfies that criterion (1177b 21). It might seem, and incautious commentators have often suggested, that this emphasis on self-sufficiency fits in badly with the claims in the discussions of friendship that it is an essential part of the good life and that nobody would choose to live without friends

It should be noted that Aristotle explicitly discusses these doubts, in Book IX, Chapter 9. What of the contention that the self-sufficient man has no need of friends (1169b 5)? Having reiterated the importance and value of friends, Aristotle makes the distinction that he needs. The life of the contemplative man needs few external goods, so such a man will have little need of 'friendships of utility', of business associations; the life of such a man is also intrinsically pleasant, so he will not need companions to keep him amused. Thus, his main occupation in life can go on without dependence on other people to aid him. This is the way

Aristotle tells us, in which the *eudaemon* life is self-sufficient. But we must not forget that contemplation is the dominant theme, not the whole, of the good life. The requirement of possessing friends is no more incompatible with the sort of self-sufficiency that Aristotle has in mind than is the requirement of being reasonably good-looking, and more important by far.

Some of Aristotle's discussions of the matters dealt with in this chapter bear the mark of their date. Jane Austen's portrayal of social relationships also bear the mark of its date. But only a very unsympathetic reader will on that account find what these authors have to say without value. Readers of these two books of the *Nicomachean Ethics* are sometimes inclined to dismiss them as unimportant because they do not link up closely with the main arguments of the work. But for Aristotle, who views ethics as the preface to politics, the discussion of these social relationships on a smaller canvas than the complete political scene is an essential part of the grand design. We shall not have a complete account of Aristotle's view of the life of man without taking into account the discussions of the *Politics* as well.

10

Eudaemonia

From our survey of Aristotle's ethical theory so far, it seems clear that eudaemonia is something highly complex. We are told that it requires good looks, good birth and reasonable wealth; of these the last, wealth, may seem merely a necessary aid to eudaemonia rather than a part of it, but this is not so of good looks and good birth. These are, no doubt, comparatively minor requirements; more importantly, all the excellences, whether of character or of intelligence, are specifically stated to be of value in themselves – even practical wisdom, though important as providing the context for theoretical contemplation, is also to be valued for itself (1144a 1–2). What we find in the *Nicomachean Ethics* we also find elsewhere. Thus, in the *Rhetoric* (1360b 9) Aristotle speaks of eudaemonia and its parts, and we have already quoted the *Magna Moralia* as saying that eudaemonia is composed of many goods. But, apart from these specific assertions of the complexity of eudaemonia, one might well think it strange that such a large proportion of the discussion should be devoted to these other matters if they played no, or only a minor, role in the good life.

On the other hand, even in Book I Aristotle has said that the three commonly accepted candidates for being the *eudaemon* life are those of sensual pleasure, of political activity and of contemplation, though he dismisses the life of sensual pleasure from consideration pretty abruptly. At least verbally, this strongly suggests that Aristotle thinks of eudaemonia as being comprised in one single dominant activity. When we come to the latter part of Book X of the *Nicomachean Ethics* it at least appears that

Aristotle says that the most *eudaemon* life is the life of contemplation and the second most *eudaemon* life is the political life. This,
not surprisingly, leads many readers to conclude that Aristotle
has forgotten what he has said elsewhere and is identifying
eudaemonia with what he regards as the best component in life
and not with the good life as a whole. One is at least tempted to
say that, in consistency with the general tenor of his work,
Aristotle should have said that eudaemonia was a life in which all
human excellences and all worthwhile activities were given full
expression and in which no human excellence was left atrophied
by neglect, even if contemplation was to be emphasized as being
an important and even dominant constituent.

It is perhaps impossible not to think that in claiming that the
most *eudaemon* life will be devoted as exclusively to the contemplation of eternal and necessary truths as the feebleness of human
nature will permit, Aristotle has shown too much enthusiasm for
his own profession, but it is not clear that he has altogether
changed the question at issue. Speaking in modern terms, in
choosing a career, in choosing one's hobbies and leisure pursuits,
one is inevitably limiting other activities in one's life, but not
totally excluding them. The person who decides to become a
physician has not decided to give up eating. So within an
inclusive conception of eudaemonia, the good life, we must
inevitably also select some dominant activity or activities. One
cannot, for example, decide to be a brain surgeon in one's spare
time; it requires dedication. So it is not perhaps unreasonably
charitable to Aristotle to take his verbal identification of contemplation with eudaemonia in the latter chapters of Book X to be
the selection of a dominant feature within a life containing other
elements necessary to full eudaemonia. In this connection we
must not forget, as some commentators have done, that while
emphasizing the self-sufficiency of the life of contemplation,
Aristotle has already explained in his discussion of friendship that
the self-sufficiency is to be construed as independence from aid
and amusement, not from the companionship of true friends.

There are two further questions that require discussion. The
first of these is why Aristotle should select the life of political
activity and the life of contemplation as the only dominant

features worthy of consideration as constituents in a good life; the second is why he should come down so heavily in favour of the life of contemplation, and to understand this, one needs information beyond what is explicitly said in the *Nicomachean Ethics*.

There is no profound philosophical reason why Aristotle singles out only two ways of life as worth serious consideration for the dominant role in the eudaemon life. He is reflecting the social values of his time and of the upper classes into which he was not born but with which he was associated throughout his life. As among the slave owners of the southern states and aristocratic Englishmen of the eighteenth and earlier nineteenth centuries, a trade or even a profession was not seriously considered among aristocrats of ancient Greece. One might play the lyre in an amateur way (but not the aulos, which was professionally played, often by women of easy virtue); Plato consistently expressed his scorn for those who accepted money for teaching; Dionysius, the tyrant of Syracuse, was a playwright, but he paid to have his plays put on the stage. Rather as the Hon. Robert Boyle and even King Charles II had their chemistry laboratories in the late seventeenth century for disinterested experiment, so in ancient Greece the unpaid life of the savant was respectable, but most upper-class men, like eighteenth-century aristocrats in England, devoted themselves to public affairs. It is doubtful whether it could even have occured to an aristocratic Greek of Aristotle's time to wonder whether the life, say, of a painter or a nurse might be yet more rewarding than Aristotle's own two candidates. There can be no doubt that Aristotle's audience was at least mainly composed of members of the slave-owning classes who shared these aristocratic views without question. It is hard to think that the admiring characterization of the great-souled or proud man in Chapter 3 of Book IV could have been addressed to any other audience.

Our second question was why Aristotle should so emphatically select the life of contemplation as pre-eminently the most *eudaemon*. He tells us that the life of contemplation is most like the life of God and that god is the supremely *eudaemon* being. He says that we should not heed those who say that, being men, we should think of human things: 'so far as possible one should act as an immortal and strive to live according to the highest in oneself (1177b 33–34). This will be more intelligible if we understand better what Aristotle means by contemplation and how he conceives of the life of God.

Theoretical wisdom, we were told, in Book VI, is excellence in the field of knowledge of things necessary and unchanging. We were there told that such knowledge must start with intuitive reason, a kind of intellectual perception that grasps first principles (1142a 26). From these first principles the wise man proceeds to draw deductive inferences; traditional Euclidean geometry is laid out as starting from axioms and deducing theorems from them in this way. Contemplation is the exercise of that excellence that is theoretical wisdom. It is essentially an activity, not a process. Contemplation is complete in itself at any time and has no limit ouside itself; if one contemplates the incommensurability of the side and diagonal of a square (one of Aristotle's favourite examples), only boredom, weariness or other business will interrupt the contemplation; contemplation does not develop and reach completion when it must necessarily stop. Thus, strictly speaking, proving the incommensurability of the side and the diagonal is not contemplation, but rather a process which must terminate with a QED. Contemplation proper is the enjoyment, not the acquisition, of knowledge. Proving, in which one proceeds from the previously known to deduce further truths, is clearly a process and thus is not, strictly speaking, contemplation. This is a point to which we shall have to return.

God, as Aristotle conceives of God, is pure intuitive reason. God is intuitive reason, not its possessor. This is made quite clear in the *Metaphysics* and the *Physics*. It is said, but less clearly, in the *Nicomachean Ethics*, for the translation at 1096a 24–25 should be: 'God, i.e., intuitive reason', not 'God and intuitive reason'. As pure intuitive reason, God has no concern with the world of becoming. The world of becoming and process, in which we live when not engaged in contemplation, is the object of the senses that depend on possession of a body. This world is not fully intelligible, since it is not necessary and unchanging but is imperfect, imperfect because it is always changing for better or worse. We should not think of God's unawareness of the world of becoming as a limitation; the supremely *eudaemon* and blessed being will concern itself only with the most worthwhile objects, which will make his activity the most perfect and therefore the most pleasant (1174b 22–23). Aristotle even says that God, in contemplating the most worthy objects, must contemplate himself. This is difficult, but seems to mean that there is no ultimate distinction between reason and its objects. 'In a way, reason is potentially the objects of reason' (*On the Soul* 408b 18). The awareness of necessary truth is not to be easily distinguished from necessary truth itself. Aristotle finds laughable the notion of the gods displaying the excellences that men, with their bodily needs and nonrational emotion, display: how can the gods be brave, temperate or just? To think of them that way is anthropomorphism; gods do not have nonrational emotions to display in a mean disposition nor have they bodily needs. In this context 'gods' appears in the plural immediately above; but philosophically Aristotle, like Plato who also from time to time spoke of 'gods' in the plural, was surely a monotheist. We also must not think that God cannot prove theorems and is limited to contemplation of the known; God has no need to prove. Proof is a process from ignorance to knowledge, but God's knowledge is always perfect. The need for process must be a sign of imperfection; what is perfect is unchanging.

Now man has only a limited capacity, but a capacity, for intuitive reason. Since intuitive reason is in man and God is intuitive reason there is a divine element in man (1177b 28). Man as a human being is mortal and ends with his bodily death, since his functions are in general dependent on his body. But, in Aristotle's view, intuitive reason, unlike the senses and the emotions, is independent of the body. As divine, it is immortal: 'Intuitive reason seems to enter into us as a substance and to be imperishable', he says in *On the Soul* (408b 18). It seems, though Aristotle does not anywhere to my knowledge expressly say so, that there is just one divine intuitive reason in which men partake, not that there are many intuitive reasons, each belonging to a different man, separate from the divine reason and merely akin to it. There is in us a divine element, not something resembling it. Because the divine is not spatially located it is able to be present in all men.

It is easy to be surprised that Aristotle should insist so strongly on contemplation as the highest good, seeming to leave room for the display of other excellences only when one is too tired for contemplation. But we must not think that the kind of position that Aristotle is here advocating is in itself unusual. While Aristotle rejects Plato's form of the good on technical grounds, he is following Plato in seeing the highest eudaemonia in contemplation of what Plato called the real world outside the cave. The neo-Platonists, Plotinus and his followers, were in the same tradition of aiming to transcend the world of becoming for the sake of the world of being. The mystics of all ages and all traditions, eastern and western, differing, no doubt, from Aristotle in many important ways, still agree with him in putting forward the contemplative life as the most valuable and the most blissful.

But, even so, the down-to-earth element in Aristotle is apparent in this discussion. It is hard to believe that any Christian contemplative has justified his choice of a way of life by claiming that as such he is more self-sufficient (1177a 27) and his activities less expensive (1178a 24), as Aristotle does.

But there remain difficulties in understanding Aristotle's position that we must consider. In the first place, if Aristotle is merely advocating a dominant place for contemplation in life, it is hard to see why he should go to the extremes he does. Thus, he says that only tiredness and other human weaknesses should limit one's concentration on contemplation. I can offer no satisfactory explanation of this.

In the second place, the life of God is one strictly of contemplation in the narrow sense. God is intuitive reason, and as such does not engage in proof; also none of his knowledge will be derived knowledge gained by proof. One must presume that this is not a limitiation of God's knowledge, but rather that God is able to see immediately by intuitive reason what man can, at best, acquire by proof. But clearly intuitive reason in man is much more limited in scope, in Aristotle's view. At best men can directly intuit the basic truths on which a science is built and must then construct that science by argument from these basic principles. But in many sciences, as Aristotle himself admits

(1095a 32 ff), we have to begin elsewhere, from what is not intuitively evident, and attempt to work towards the intuitively evident. It would seem, then, that if man is to limit himself to contemplation in the strict sense, he will lead a very impoverished intellectual life. In his discussion of theoretical reasoning in Book VI Aristotle in fact gives a much wider interpretation of contemplation including the process of proof and the knowledge acquired thereby; intuitive reason is only the starting point. But if we thus extend the notion of contemplation we must face the fact that it is no longer solely, or even primarily, the exercise of the divine element of intuitive reason which is the activity of God. We shall, for the most part, be engaged in a human, not a divine, type of contemplation. Once again, I have no ready solution to offer to this difficulty.

The matter is further exacerbated by a difficulty that we noted in passing in earlier chapters. The difficulty is that, even if we extend the notion of contemplation to cover proof and derived knowledge, the statement of axioms and the deduction of conclusions from them plays an extremely minor role in Aristotle's own published works. A large proportion of Aristotle's works are biological and based on long and careful observation; the ethical and political works, and the vast collection of descriptions of the constitutions of various states, a collection largely lost, are clearly not based on intuitive premisses; even the most fundamental works of philosophy, such as the *Metaphysics* and the *Physics*, are largely devoted to the discussion of puzzles and problems and contain little deduction. But while those fundamental philosophical works might be said to lack the form of a deductive science only because they are still imperfect, it is difficult to believe that any such view can be taken of the biological works, while Aristotle has said over and over again that the aim of the *Nicomachean Ethics* is not theoretical but practical. It would seem, then, that if we are to attribute to Aristotle a choice of the kind of life that he tells us that we should choose, we have to extend the notion of contemplation yet further, so that it will not be recognizable as that which is outlined in Book VI. The life of contemplation is now merely the life of the scholar as opposed to that of the man of affairs. But if we choose this interpretation, the imitation of God, that played so large a part in Aristotle's argument, has receded still further into the background. Once again, I have no solution to offer to this difficulty.

The final difficulty that I shall raise is really one that encapsulates the others. Chapter 8 of Book X ends with a paean of praise for the life of the man of theoretical wisdom. Chapter 9 begins as follows: 'If then these matters, the excellences, friendship and pleasure have been sufficiently discussed in outline, has our undertaking reached its goal? Or, as they say, is the goal in practical matters not to contemplate each matter and understand it, but rather to do it?' Here Aristotle explicitly rejects contemplation as the goal of his enquiry; it would seem that in so doing he is distracting us from what in the previous chapters he has said should occupy our best energies. There is surely no solution to all these difficulties. We must agree that Aristotle has let his enthusiasm get the better of him in his discussion of the theoretical life and replace his extreme claims with the more moderate view that the life of the scholar is the most choiceworthy, only in the sense that it is the best career to choose, not as the sole constituent in the good life.

It should be noted that, in a way that resembles and perhaps echoes Plato's claim for the life of his philosopher kings, Aristotle claims that the life of contemplation is the most pleasant of all lives. Aristotle certainly thinks that there is a very close link between worth and pleasantness. Pleasure is also valuable in itself; nobody thinks that one should have an ulterior motive for seeking pleasure (1172b 22). But, if hedonism is the doctrine that pleasure is the sole good, then Aristotle explicitly rejects hedonism; he endorses Plato's argument (*Philebus* 21–22) that pleasure cannot be the sole good, since pleasure with wisdom is better than pleasure without wisdom. According to Aristotle, an activity is more pleasant if it is more worthwhile, not more worthwhile if it is more pleasant.

Aristotle does recognize the life of activity in the state, exercising one's ethical excellences, as a form of eudaemonia; but it is clearly for him a second choice. Within such a life he does not recognize that 'the daily round and common task should furnish all we ought to ask'. Such a life is more rewarding, more *eudaemon*, if one accomplishes great things, and for that one needs money and power. For that reason the man of affairs is more a hostage to fortune than the contemplative scholar. A life, Aristotle holds, is more worthwhile if full of accomplishments than if it fails to display the more aristocratic excellences. This will seem repugnant to some modern readers, but they should face the facts and try to understand even if they disagree.

The work ends, as we have already noticed, with a further claim that in ethics it is not theory but action that matters. But while theoretical discussion may not be the end, it is certainly thought by Aristotle to be a means towards the goal. If we understand more about the nature of excellence of character, of legitimate excuses, of wisdom theoretical and practical, of the nature of weakness of will, all to the good, but this understanding is not something to be prized simply for its own sake; it is knowledge which should help the legislator to frame better laws that will better lead and compel men towards a good life. Aristotle's audience was composed of able young men of influential families, the legislators of the future. He has presupposed the members of his audience to be well brought up; moreover, they are young men who are going to be for the most part leading men of affairs, not scholars. The aim of the *Nicomachean Ethics* is practical, not as trying to improve the character of his well-brought-up audience, but as giving them the sort of understanding that leaders of society need. One can behave well enough if one has been well trained, but to establish the laws that are needed to ensure that the young are well-brought-up, some insight is needed into human behaviour. This is why Aristotle regards his *Ethics* as the preliminary to his lectures on politics. 'Must we not go on to consider next whence and how a person may become a lawmaker?' (1180b 28–29). The last sentence of the *Nicomachean Ethics* has the form of an opening sentence of a set of lectures on politics; it is there that the question of the best form of political organization, that which will enable citizens to live the good life, and the more detailed questions that follow from it, will be discussed. If the reader has noticed an absence of discussion of the principles that should govern our relationships with one another, such as would be central in a modern ethical work, it is because in Aristotle's view, such issues belong to politics proper, not to ethics.

Further Reading

GENERAL INTRODUCTIONS TO ARISTOTLE

J.L. Ackrill *Aristotle the Philosopher* (Oxford, 1981).

J. Barnes *Aristotle* (Oxford, 1982).

BOOKS ON ARISTOTLE'S ETHICS

W.F.R. Hardie: *Aristotle's Ethical Theory;* 2nd ed. (Oxford, 1980)

J. Barnes, M. Schofield and R.Sorabji (eds) *Articles on Aristotle: Ethics and Politics;* (London, 1977)

A.O. Rorty (ed.), *Essays on Aristotle's Ethics*, (Berkeley, 1980).

Index